CHAMBERET

CHAMBERET

Recollections from an Ordinary Childhood

Claude Morhange-Bégué

*Translated from French
by Austryn Wainhouse*

The Marlboro Press / Marlboro, Vermont

For Vanessa

CHAMBERET

Recollections from an Ordinary Childhood

Writing about my childhood today, I have come to see that those were not ordinary times. But for me, as a child, they were; for I had not known any others.

Since then, those unbearable times have gone on recurring here and there in too many places, for too many children.

1

When I was not quite eight years old they came and took my mother from me. There were three German officers of indefinite color and a little old woman all in black, perhaps wearing something white on her head; but I'm not sure about the white, it could be that I am making it up because it goes with a type, the peasant woman in characteristic head-dress. Three officers in gray-green and a little old woman in black, a wizened old Corrèze countrywoman whom I didn't know; but who had however stood and pointed straight at the house I had just left and could no longer see, being right then in the one adjoining it, looking out at the road through the loosely criss-crossed pattern of the crochet work curtain hanging in the window.

And she had stood and pointed to the house where I ordinarily lived, the Doctor's house, metal gate painted black, brickwork framing it, with my father's brass plate still there, a plate such as you see in the city although we were in the country, giving his office hours–the first mark of the difference between the world of the city where he had always lived, and the rural world, unknown, fraught with pitfalls, where he had come and met his death.

And when I had walked into my school classroom, just as I did every morning, a great silence had overspread everything, invading the pale gray of the walls opposite me, the faces turned toward me, all the eyes looking at me, the faces all looking at me, my schoolmates' faces and those of the two teachers–while ordinarily there was but one. That silence: I write it and write it again, wanting the words which recreate it in its reality, wanting also a sure idea of the exact order of events, the hands that took me by the shoulders and gently, firmly turned me around toward the door I had just entered by and through which I must now go back out, this instant, but calmly, without a fuss; wanting a recollection of the words that must have been spoken to me–and spoken to me by who else but the teacher?– giving me instructions to go, to clear out at once, to escape. For today, thirty years later, I realize that it was by the skin of my teeth I got away then, with my mother in the classroom across the hall, already under arrest and lying with might and main to try to save her only offspring whom the neighbors, to get her off their hands, have packed straight off to school like any other morning, to school where the three classes have today been made up into two because the third classroom, that of the upper grades, is being temporarily used as a jail by these gentlemen from the *Das Reich* division who have with utmost formality just arrested my mother upon the denunciation of her colleague, the other doctor in the village, and who, courteously, but resolutely, begin to question her to find out where the child is. The child is me, and there I am, a few paces away, within an enveloping silence that fills the four walls, rises to the white ceiling up there, and sinks back down. I am standing just inside the door I have not as yet closed behind me, with, at my side or a step to the rear like the woman who follows the man in the bas-reliefs from Upper Egypt, the little Balard girl, the little neighbor whose parents sent me off, the Doctor once arrested, to follow in her footsteps and share her fate, as on any other morning walking up the road that runs through the village–the one, no question about it, upon which the car with her in it has just driven away. Just, for I don't remember having stayed very long at the Balards' after the scene I watched through the window, the window they drew me away from, taking me by the shoulders, calmly, firmly.

And when I arrive at school, as usual dawdling my way thither alongside the little neighbor, she is already in that room, ten yards away from me, I who am still unaware that she has just been arrested and perhaps still unaware of what that really signifies (I will find out that same day, informed by the panic flight of my body refusing to share her fate); I who now would still be capable of rushing after her shrieking *Maman!* and overtaking her and casting myself into the refuge of her arms and into the jaws of the wolf. She is very near by, her questioners civil but stubborn, pressing her to disclose the whereabouts of the child whose presence she is denying. The child is there, on the other side of the hallway, stupidly sent into the trap she has now to be got out of, immediately, calmly. For I resemble my mother. And it is amidst perfect calm that I leave the school, surrounded by continuing silence and by emptiness–and writing about it today I wish to pay homage to those women, to the two teachers, to the town clerk, to the dressmaker, who there and then improvise a rescue scheme, put together in haste but coolly and which will work–; silence and emptiness enfolding me still, crossing the deserted village square; nothing, no one there except for one woman and a child; anonymous space into which no eye gazes, for there is no one at the windows and no one in the shops; a flat and infinite surface upon which only two vertical shapes move, the black and white checkerboard of a back surmounted by a vertical black and white chignon, and, fifty feet behind, following her but pretending to have no connection with her, I who hie myself calmly away towards escape, towards safety.

Eight or ten years later the chance discovery of a painting–a Chirico, I believe–, black and white checkerboard surrounded by arcades and buildings, utterly blank facades, utterly empty and gleaming space against which rises, the sole vertical there, the striding silhouette of a man–will fill me with a fright I do not understand at the time and that becomes clearer today in this attempt to reconstruct, to put into words something that there is no name for but which lies within human grasp all the same.

When we got back to the house belonging to that Marie of the back and the chignon, my aunt and my grandmother were there; it seems to me they hugged me in their arms and were crying. I do not remember any words being addressed to me; I can't say now whether anything was said at all, whether they explained that my mother had been taken away and that I wasn't likely to see her for a while or even ever again. From within the great emptiness that filled me there does indeed arise one sentence, be it actual memory or phantasm: *Your mother has been arrested*; but from where do I get the incontrovertible knowledge of the gravity of her plight when I look about to find myself–and this I do clearly remember–lying in a big white bed, white counterpane, vast white eiderdown, repeating to the rhythm of the clock whose pendulum my eyes are following on the wall across the room: *She-will-come-back, she-won't-come-back, she-will-come-back, she-won't-come-back?*

I can endeavor today to fill in the gaps, to imagine the wait of the two women, my aunt and grandmother, first going off along the Upper Road *(I'm going to drop the little one off and I'll rejoin you,* my mother must have told them, but those are my words and I have no idea what hers were) and not seeing anything happen, and then later, a little afterward, going to where the meeting was supposed to be, two persons instead of the three who ought to have been there. I can try to imagine the moment when they decide to leave their temporary shelter, the bush by the turn of the road, acknowledging or else–I don't know–refusing to acknowledge the meaning of the fifteen or twenty minutes that have elapsed without my mother appearing–my mother, their sister, their daughter. I can try to imagine the subsequent conversation with Marie, the dressmaker, who hurries off to the village, seeking news. She must cross the already deserted square that everybody has fled, out of precaution, for in Limousin of late the deeds of the *Das Reich* people have been murderous, word has got around; fled also in order not to see, in order not to be seen seeing the return of the little automobile, red or gray-green, which drove from the town hall straight to our house and which returns with the three German officers and in addition the fair-haired woman doctor, informed upon by her colleague, the Vichyite mayor of the village, whose name–it was Le Seigneur–has gone to his head and who arrogates to himself the right to do away with the foreigner, the competitor, the *maquisarde.* As if a township of a thousand souls did not provide enough ailing bodies to enable two physicians to earn their livings and get along together! As if one could not have different ideas without having to kill each other!

In order to see nothing at all, in order not to have to admit that one had seen. For to see and to do nothing, even if there is nothing to be done, is in a certain way to participate, to become accomplice. The accomplice of the victim and of the killers too. To see without protesting–one can certainly understand that, for right here and right now power is all on the side of the SS and there is no longer anything anyone can do for my mother, trapped by her own heroism, and who must now ready herself for a very long descent into that land whence it is supposed no one returns. But to see without suffering, to see without imagining oneself in the shoes of her upon whom the vise is closing, to see without sympathizing, that is quite another story, and nobody, except those who are going to set to work to save us, wishes to implicate himself to that point.

She—Marie, the dressmaker, of checkered blouse and gray chignon—crosses the already deserted square and arrives at the school just after I do. For, in the silence of the classroom that I have entered unconcernedly, in the everyday way, the way I enter every morning, I only situate her behind me as I come to a confused halt in the middle of the room, fetching up against the denseness of that silence, against the unanimous incredulity of those gazes fastened upon me. But without understanding as yet, and taking hardly any notice of the conference in progress behind me: upon my entering, one of the teachers had risen, coming toward me as if to forbid me access to my school; and while, having moved past her, I stand there before the faces watching me, she takes me by the shoulders—while at the same moment, and behind me, the other teacher is whispering, probably with Marie, who has just come in.

Those two women, my aunt and my grandmother, waiting for the dressmaker they sent to find out what was happening and who returns with the child—what did they say upon beholding me? Did they realize simply upon seeing me—who according to the original

plan was not supposed to be there but under cover at
the Balards' next door to where we lived–simply upon
seeing me did they realize that she whom they were
waiting for and had waited for in vain on the Upper
Road and who hadn't come, was not about to come,
was perhaps not going to return? Or is it a nod on
Marie's part, a gesture of her hand, a movement of her
arm that transmits the sinister news to them? I remember something passing from them to me, I remember
my grandmother exclaiming, getting ready to wail and
my aunt *relieved*, relieved to see me; which, in retro-
spect, explains to me that at not seeing my mother
come up the Upper Road they had feared not only for
her but for me, for me hidden in the house adjoining
the one where they had just arrested my mother and
from which I had almost been able to see them take her
away.

Those two women, my aunt and my grandmother–
what then did they say when they saw me? To the elder
I want to ascribe some of the words she was to
pronounce later on: *Something awful has befallen us*,
while my aunt hushes her, relieved that just one has
been caught, and not two. I would like to talk about her
arms enfolding me, offering me protection, comfort, in
the role that is constantly hers during the absence of
her for whose return I begin, at that precise instant, to
wait. I visualize the scene: the two women side by side
and then face to face and I close to them, at the right
angle of the triangle we three form, and Marie, our
saviour–in those days people were shot and hanged for
less–standing behind me, a step or so away, always in

the background. The scene is dimly lit, in shadow; above all, it is mute. I no longer know what was said to me, I no longer know how it was said. And the unshaped phrase that rises in me: *But she is going to return, have to wait for her, be patient,* I may perhaps have invented it to explain the inexorable *She-will-come-back/she-won't-come-back* being told to me by the clock on the wall at the foot of the broad white bed, a bed for grown-ups, for two, whose entire horizontal part is white and infinite in its extent whereas the three walls to either side and ahead, with the clock ticking on one of them, close in upon me when I begin to count: *Will-come-back, won't-come-back, will-come-back, won't-come-back.*

Ten minutes before eight: that is the time that remains in my memory, and whether it is a possible time, a plausible one, or whether I have imagined it, I do not know. I also see the hands showing eight-thirty. Today I do not know why they put me to bed nor what they could have told me to justify putting me to bed in daytime. I remember the half-light, the white bed occupying the alcove, the swinging of the pendulum. I am alone in the alcove which appears full of light by contrast with the obscurity of the rest of the room where the shutters must have been drawn. I do not know where the adults are—Marie whose bed I am in, my aunt, my grandmother; somewhere in the tiny dwelling there is also an aged woman, Marie's mother. I think I saw her before they put me to bed, a squat, black-clad shape, and kindly, good-hearted—*My poor child* and the others whispering to her to keep quiet—

and her saying something about a good hot cup of lime-blossom tea. Left alone in the big bed with the enormous white counterpane, how do I adjust to the thought that my mother has been taken away from me? Your mother has been arrested, she is going to return home after a certain while. All that appears clear to me is that then and there, in that place, I begin not to feel anything: I say nothing, I do not cry, I do not scream. I am there by myself, lying full length amidst the whiteness, with the pendulum rhythmically repeating *will-come-back, won't-come-back*. It's not a question of a game, of a verbal simulation by means of which the freshly sustained hurt may be dominated; but of a decree of fate, of a kind of divine judgment that I beg from the unknown powers of chance. Every quarter of an hour the clock strikes: once, twice, then three times, then four, and gives me a response. Sometimes the sharp note falls upon *will-come-back*, sometimes upon *won't-come-back*. Whichever it is, I start again, to invalidate, to confirm. On that morning of April 8, 1944, I become superstitious, totally so and for quite some time. I, the little Jewish girl, with my atheistic background and rationalist upbringing, still unacquainted with any super-terrestrial power, I invent God the Father right off the bat in order to entrust to him and to haggle with him about that which is to come: the return of my mother. In time with the pendulum I start an unending interrogation of the auguries; for those who know may also be mistaken. And if the chime sounds an affirmative *will-come-back*, it is never for anything but fifteen minutes and the next fifteen minutes may throw everything into question again. And if those fifteen minutes confirm, the following fifteen may undo everything. In short, I suddenly learn what doubt is, a form of skepticism which can also beget hope. For the inverse process is also true and two *won't-come-backs* in a row can be cancelled out by the *will-come-back* which succeeds them. I stay there a long time, a long time. I do not know where the adults are or what they are doing. I am shut up inside a white eternity animated only by the wall clock. Within my field of vision, neither door nor window. I remain as if turned to stone upon the beachlike white expanse of the bed. I have no desire to get up. I do not sleep, I don't even shift position. Stretched out, I contemplate the wall and listen to the clock, trying to decipher its forever repeated message. I have no idea when or how I got out of that bed.

The park, the park belonging to the Maisonneuve estate, where I betrayed my mother. The park behind its grillwork enclosure, halfway between my house and school–the girls' school, the boys' school, Marie on the square where you also have the grocer, the pharmacy, the hotel, the shop belonging to the shoemaker whose daughter with blond braids is my friend. The park with the high grillwork, painted in my mind's eye, and, behind the grillwork, a tall hedge of bushes with long shiny leaves, then an upward-sloping lawn, some triangular-shaped yews, a white, more or less classical facade, and maybe a pediment. Beyond, an unknown world to which I have never given any thought but whose bordering hedge returns to run along the Upper

Road when you take the short cut to go to Marie's house, which has two entrances, a village entrance on a little street near the square where the church is, and the other entrance by way of the garden, off the road that leads to the fairgrounds above the village and outside it. A topography that shows some unsteadiness but containing fixed landmarks, the squares and the main streets leading to them, the Eymoutiers Road where I live, the Treignac Road where there is a garden, one of the gardens where I got my fondness for those roses that bloom too fully and dry out and then suddenly fall to pieces, dead already, giant tea-roses with speckled pistils, blaze of poppy-red roses, rich clusters of tiny little long-lasting roses, and so on; this immoderate fondness of mine for excessive flowers, too large, sometimes of too bright a color, sometimes gaudy, sometimes too numerous, mismatched, chubby peonies and especially giant dahlias which paradoxically turn out to be the same flower as the smaller so-called boule-de-neige, crinkled like the puckers on the front of one of my dresses, exuberantly colored too but of milder hues, little pastel squares juxtaposed; this fondness for bushes that produce edible fruit, currant, raspberry, gooseberry bushes of which at home I always eat the still unripe berries (oh, the juicy and at the same time tart-tasting gooseberries that have not yet had time to lose flavor in ripening) up until the day when a pearl-gray garden snake wrapped in tight coils around the bush's four stalks made me run away shrieking towards my mother's protecting arms; and the abundance, the multiplicity of too closely spaced varieties with their dizzyingly competing colors and shapes and sometimes with arresting names: snapdragons, foxgloves... A road where you also find, but a lot farther on, amidst a stand of tall larches whose arrow-straight trunks serve to make telephone poles, wooden poles become gray under repeated rains, not so high as the one that's like a concrete ladder with a collar of steel spikes around it about six feet up off the ground in front of my house between where my garden is and the rosebush my mother planted there–, a road where you also find the Passade chateau where we sometimes go, the whole family together, to listen to music and to picnic on Sunday afternoons. I remember a huge rectangular table and, even more distinctly, records, stored like books on pine shelves covering one entire wall of the room. During the three winters we spent in this village we listened to side after side of those old-fashioned records: the music we heard, through the frequent interruptions an improved technology has done away with today, was all Bach, admired by the owner of the collection to the exclusion of all other composers. Another road, where the post office was, where the notary's house was, led to another garden, for me an earthly paradise despite its more modest dimensions and less spectacular architecture. In the spring, after she came back to us, to celebrate her presence and her birthday, that is where I went to pick two enormous bouquets and I can see them still, great crazy bouquets of wet flowers that after school I bring home hidden behind my back and hide under my grandmother's bed until the next day. That country childhood is brimming with flowers: the primroses in our garden, primroses of pale and scarcely differentiated colors which upon close inspection prove tinted with a tiny amount of parme or else acid yellow, the hydrangeas whose colors are revived by sprinkling the ground underneath with bits of slate, the tall tiger lilies that leave a golden dust upon your nose, an oppressive syringea, a bush with whitish globes which become pulpy between my fingers before dissolving into a sticky liquid, and the rosebushes, the one planted by my mother, city-dweller and beginner, stem cutting popped in the ground that, by magic, takes root and blooms in velvety purple flowers, and the rosebush belonging to me, mine in name only, already woven into the meshes of the chicken wire on top of the cement wall separating us from the road, and producing pink clumps amidst which, one day, I clip off a very small branch, having seen my mother, dressed in black, a purple rose in her hand, about to take it to the place where my father lies. And I give her my little clump to take too, though it isn't very clear to me where my father is, lacking as I then do the words and the images which denominate and illustrate death.

And in the intervals between these fixed points of reference, blurred spaces, paths with a definite beginning and end but which over the rest of their course oscillate, in my memory, between neighboring and contiguous temptations, between logical impossibilities, unprecise territories, pseudopodic in form, which shift in defiance of topographical likelihood. So it was with the Maisonneuve park, situated on the Eymoutiers Road, before whose grillwork gate I once saw, at the time of a 15th of August procession, a temporary altar heaped with roses, more dazzling for being totally unexplained; but abutting also on the Upper Road and adjoining Marie's garden, since it was from there we entered it during that day, perhaps at the end of the morning, proceeding to ensconce ourselves in the most visible and hence most improbable of spots, on the grounds surrounding the chateau of a Petainist, a small manufacturer from Brive or Limoges who rarely comes there, and where, so these women who are saving us must have said to one another, nobody would dream of looking. For in the event of a thorough search, troops posted throughout the village, everybody out of the house and into the street, we all risk death, locked into the church as at Oradour, hanged from the balconies as at Tulle, shot point-blank as in three-quarters of Europe. And if at that moment and for a few weeks' time Tulle and Oradour still only refer to a quiet village and a sleepy town strung out along a river where even the firearms factory had brought us but one alert when we were living there, wailing sirens, guardian collapsing upon the body of the child rushing up the hill and whom she strives to protect, if Tulle and Oradour do not yet perpetuate the names of massacres still to be committed, nobody here is unaware that the Germans trouble themselves very little about those who take it into their heads to resist them—not even I who, one evening earlier, happening to wake up, overheard a muffled conversation between my mother and my uncle back from a clandestine trip to somewhere

dangerous, in it singling out, by the anxiety it gener-
ated, its tone, its context, the silence following it, the
word *deported*, soon thereafter come upon at the
conclusion of a volume from the Bibliothèque Rose
collection I was then devoted to.

Today I no longer know how or at what point, with
what words or what absence of words, they got me out
of that big white bed, how the three of us left, two
women and a child and breeders of the plague all three,
led by the anodine shape in checkered black and white,
Marie, slight of figure, of unobtrusive aspect, in perpet-
ual half-mourning for I know not what father, husband,
brother, fiancé, who with her work as a seamstress
supports her mother, an old woman completely in
black and probably a half cripple, and who, when the
time comes, reveals herself a woman with a clever
head on her shoulders, steers me out of school under
the very nose of those who are trying to get hold of me,
shelters me in her house throughout the worst of the
day's danger, then directs us into the park belonging to
the chateau: greensward, green space irregularly
planted with yews and shrubbery.

I remember or I imagine–and this hesitation irritates
me–that we steal from one patch of garden to another,
screened by the bushes in between, with Marie keeping
a look-out and telling us when to go. And we remain in
the park, under no cover but hidden from sight behind
something or other up until the moment, clear in my
memory, when we have to forsake that spot on the
open grass in order to reach three evergreens, spruces,
closely set trees of a good size to hide behind, one for

each of us, the child, the adult, the elder whose lives are at stake in this game as are, through implication, the lives of the others, not all of whom possess the little pepper-and-salt woman's self-collected and efficient heroism. Like, for example, the Balards, quick to unload the little flatlander girl, Jewish to boot, daughter and niece of members of the Resistance, a child come from elsewhere whose mere presence (notwithstanding my mother's assertion when she entrusted me to them: *And there's no danger in it for you*), whose mere presence threatens their security, native-born people, small holders loath to get involved in anything at all and who refuse to place their lives in jeopardy to save the life of another who, besides, isn't even somebody like them.

I suppose that someone taking the Upper Road can see over the top of the hedge down into the park and that our initial hiding-place, the three of us trying to melt in amongst the bushes and to be as still as their shadows on the ground, affords inadequate protection, considering those certain persons who passing along the Upper Road and peering inside might be tempted to guarantee their own safety by designating verbally and by pointing to the three women, the three generations, who constitute the day's quarry for an SS division.

To get to the three evergreens we have to cross a broad stretch of trimmed green lawn, exposed to the eye of any eventual passerby. Once again Marie acts as look-out, a slender silhouette, our guardian angel, and she gives us the signal to advance, having probably swept her vigilant gaze over a sufficiently long segment of road to be reasonably sure we can risk the crossing of the lawn. I, who have been forewarned with I cannot imagine what words, I do know that I am very frightened, transposing the danger implied by the admonishment to silence at all cost into some secret disaster, only heightened by my failure to find any concrete image for it other than this new word associated, precisely, with a dread I can detect in the speech of the adults who employ it: the word *deported*, picked out during a night-time conversation between my uncle and my mother, afterwards come upon at the end of one the stories I have been reading and about which I truly know nothing unless it be that it rhymes with *arrested*. In the language being employed by adults– Your mother has been arrested *but* (you mustn't worry), *but* (she'll come back soon), *but* (you've got to be brave) or whatever else in that vein was inevitably said to me–appears an implicit negative structure which contradicts what I am being told and which affirms to me, the more emphatically after what I sensed of their emotion and relief upon seeing me show up in the half-lighted room, the more keenly too in that it does not stand upon words which would give it some sort of substance and perhaps provide me with some images to cling to–, which affirms to me that it is dangerous and that the chances are she really won't come back at all . . . which is what the pendulum sometimes stated earlier today: *She will come back, she won't come back*. And now, being about to dash across the flat green expanse, running the way my aunt and grandmother are running too, panic, terror before the menacing unknown, the instinct of self-preservation at whatever price, these declare themselves in me, and upon the same wave come the terms of the bargain, the hateful bargain: *Her yes but not me,* such as I will find it twenty years later in a novel which anticipates the destruction by the System of the last man: *Do it to her, not to me.*

From that day nothing subsists apart from what I have just written, no chronological reference point beyond the ones I have already given. I do not know whether we ate, drank, slept... I remember the beginning of the wait, crouching behind and in contact with the three pointed trees and trying to become one with them on this early part of an unduly warm, unduly still, unduly quiet afternoon. Crouching behind, squatting up against the tree-trunk so as to fuse with its dark mass and leave nothing for glances to settle on, forbidden to so much as stir, to speak, already prey to remorse over that convulsively formulated *Her yes but not me,* and the dread of being made to go where she has gone, of having to share her fate, a fate all the more terrifying to me because I do not know what it is and because, lacking images which would concretize it, I invent for it a horribleness stemming from all we are doing in order to save ourselves, from our unwonted behavior, from this unwonted day when for me the world has come to a stop, both time and the ordinary working of things. Time has frozen, and though it is but a number of hours, a very long afternoon we spend in the park, upon that day I catch a fleeting glimpse of eternity. Which even today makes early afternoon in the country unbearable for me, early afternoon when the summer air is too thick, too still, when a heaviness weighs on my body, when I find myself without anything to do and dare not surrender either to torpor or to seeking refuge in two reassuring arms.

Sleep may perhaps have overtaken me later on that day in the Maisonneuve park. That would have been afterward, for I do indeed remember settling down to wait, hunkering down against the tutelary tree as my aunt two yards away and my grandmother another two yards away from her were both doing, forced into inaction and immobility on the lawn with the wall or the hedge another two yards behind us and always somewhere in the background that slight figure covered with black squares and white squares, the little person whose quiet heroism simply saved our lives.

In this account must be placed something of that village, Chamberet, become my village because, taking it unthinkingly for granted, I lived my childhood there, and a happy childhood too. On certain winter mornings when I woke my bedroom window was covered with flower-patterns of frost. In my room there was my mother's big bed, then a corner fireplace where a fire was lit early in the morning. It would be cold when I had to get up, usually before the room had a chance to warm, and I am still not accustomed today to jumpings out of bed on cold mornings, to undressings which always seem premature, to that moment when, the warm nightgown removed, I would get trembling into the clothes, seemingly of ice, that lay hung over the back of the chair that served as my bedside table. After the fireplace there was the window, then my bed in the angle where two walls met, with a chair placed next to it. Then a big wardrobe. Then the door. Between the door and my mother's bed, a whole section containing I have forgotten what except for a door perhaps a third of the way along, a door to the dressing-room, a hallway equipped with a sink in front of which I fainted one day while brushing my teeth because of a tiny thread of blood coming from my mouth, possibly reminding me of what until then I had succeeded in not seeing, the battered or swollen area of a face the rest of which was a ghastly white against the sheet and white pillowcase that I had contemplated from this very same side of the room, from where I was able to observe both the candle that was lighting it and its reflection in the mirror over the mantel on the farther side of the bed.

. . . The frost-flowers on my bedroom window one morning when, perhaps sick, for I am all by myself, I try to look through them to the outside. At my height they entirely cover the glass, interlocking white peri-winkles whose petals are composed of fine veins pressed against each other the way star-shaped flowers also press against each other. One day–the same day? another day?–I discover that by rubbing my camphor chapstick upon this wintry florescence, then pressing my lips to it, I am able to brighten their pale color, and I come away quickly triumphant, my lips both red and cool. On the mornings when the monthly fair is held, through this window I watch the oxen, the calves, the pigs go by, being driven toward the fairgrounds, some of them along the main thoroughfare, some by way of the Upper Road which starts at the corner next to our house and after some twists and turns and forks winds up at the fairgrounds on the other side of Chamberet. As it is wartime, the women who have come on foot from outlying farms and hamlets–two, four, six kilometers, and at school I have classmates who do four in the morning and another four to get home, rain or shine and every day–, the women leave their sabots in the ditch at the edge of the village just before where we live, and put on the shoes they have been carrying to spare them from unnecessary wear and from the muddy roads. For it would not be right to come into town wearing sabots on the day of a fair.

. . . Before I am tucked into bed on winter nights, the humid sheets are warmed with a brick, a big rectangular glazed block, the corners rounded off, the glaze scaling off, with two holes that may be for inserting the poker or perhaps for looks or perhaps for no reason, just from tradition. Zones of brighter color, between orange and quince jelly yellow, scales that are pinker and porous, granular: I yet see the contrasting colors and texture of the brick they would heat up and then stow in my bed to dry it out and make its whiteness inviting.

The thread of events that unbearable day–I interrupted it in order to dwell upon pleasant, goodly moments, and these, as if in my despite, bring me back to something else unbearable encysted in them. That thread, I pick it up again in the barn, the Maisonneuve barn after sundown: two women and a child seated in orange canvas lawn chairs waiting for the night to pass. Actually, that barn serves as a shed, it is piled to the rafters with split firewood in which mice are gnawing away. Between these cliffs of stacked wood, two of us on one side and I on the other and still without speaking, we listen to the gnawing of the mice and the hooting of barn-owls. Barn-owls or wood-owls, the long-drawn mournful sound instills itself in me forever, bound up with the scratching of mice busy inside a woodpile. It is the first of my wakeful nights, attentive to the darkness, to the silence, to all the noises and glimmerings which compose them, tinged with the breathing of the women nearby who are asleep, who are awake, I'm not sure which; further tinged, as the years have gone by and as I have travelled, with city sounds, emergency sirens, cars, motorcycles, once a cry for help in a foreign tongue, or, in a contrary setting, the sounds of camping out, something rustling, brushing past, the cracking of a branch, once the dancing shadow of a brown bear cast upon the khaki wall of the tent; most often tinged with the breathing of a man or of a child, but always attentive, vigilant, on the alert for cries and whispers, scanning the dark.

I feel a further waning of my resources when before dawn my aunt sets out for where, several kilometers away, she will find the bus that will take her to a train that will take her to the big city to intercept my uncle before he starts homeward, toward the trap the entire Limousin has turned into. Which does not prevent him from being arrested several weeks later as he is trying to slip over the border into Spain with a view to reaching England. And from being sent to Buchenwald. And from dying within days of his return from there. But on this night of the 8th and 9th of April all that is still in the future and my aunt succeeds in her getaway, having surely hugged me and kissed me, sensible child that I am who lets out not a peep, who obeys orders not to stir and who as of then begins to keep a vigil solely for the sake of seeing everything, hearing everything, feeling everything, perhaps so that I may someday tell what these events have left behind in me and what fantasy has woven itself around them. My aunt takes leave of us and I may perhaps start right then imagining her stealthy progress, the darkness of the starry night with only a sliver of moon and the thickets of young chestnuts growing close alongside the road. She goes off and her getaway is successful: several weeks later we shall meet in Limoges, she will burst into tears at the sight of me, while I will grit my teeth and be angry at her for showing her emotion without knowing that the members of our family have already started to drop away, that the great decimation has begun.

It is barely light when my turn comes to set out. Marie is there to fetch me, then a man comes, the blacksmith, a tall man, with a craggy weatherbeaten face, rough strong hands. I walk beside him or rather beside his boots, greenish rubber boots like the ones men wear to go fishing or hunting, or else brown in color, handsome natural leather boots. Higher up than my head he has hold of my hand. Higher up than his hand and mine, very high up, his face is lit by the rays of the sun. Down here, the boots and I climb over the hills and the very high heath bushes that come up to well above my knees. His hand has firm hold of mine. Up there his face reflects the ochering light of the sun rising over the Monédières range, covered with pink heather.

I believe–from my imperfect reconstruction of events based upon what I myself remember and upon the fragmentary recollections of others, snatches of stories I chanced to overhear and which in part stuck in my mind, and were also in part deformed by me–, I believe that it was in the evening, by which time I was already in the barn, or perhaps a little before, as night was about to fall, that the Germans pulled out of Chamberet, taking the road in the direction of Treignac, passing in front of the wonderful garden, going through the woods with the tall larches, skirting the garden belonging to the Passades where we so often went for a picnic and to listen to the music of Bach on warm Sunday afternoons. They moved off toward Treignac, having been unable to get my mother to tell them where the child was, and they had her with them. From the temporary makeshift of a schoolroom jail, where it was still possible to have some illusions, and toward the official police station, which marks the beginning of her detention. Toward the prison in Limoges and toward the detention center at Drancy. Toward those months of which I know nothing other than that they are months of systematic humiliation, not having heard any stories as yet, not having ventured any questions, bound by her silence, a silence that contrasts

27

with what will come later: the daily outpouring through which, barely returned, she resurrects hell for me, who listens and absorbs the facts until I no longer discern their horror, their unacceptable character, eventually wishing in her name and behalf to undertake their telling in writing since she does not seem to want to do it, since, apparently, for the subduing of reality repeated oral recital is in her case enough, since, a few years after, this talk is becoming less frequent and she alludes to the subject only episodically, sometimes saying *All that ought to have been written down*, or, still more often and whenever one suggests that she do it: *I don't want to write about all that*, thereby leaving to me, if not the task of commemoration, at least the temptation to become the teller of things I have experienced only through her.

They move off, then, in the direction of Treignac and they take her with them, still behaving in a courteous manner toward her even though she is in their clutches, perhaps because she has light-colored hair and is Aryan in type, or because she is a doctor, or perhaps because she adjudges to herself the same dignity she unfailingly acknowledges in others. They take her away but maintain constant pressure on her: *If you are a good Frenchwoman, you should tell us where the child is.* *The child*, in their speeches to her, is without gender as was *the Doctor* when they came to arrest her and she did not see fit to profit from that imprecision in order to escape, to save her skin. My mother is unyielding; the child is not here, the child left long ago, she does not know where the child is. They bear down: *But that's not what one expects from a loving mother,* they scold; *the child would be better off with you.* Though it is a question of her own flesh and blood she manages not to give way to sentimentality, she who however has been caught because she trusted in her own invulnerability and the endless stretching time allows of, having returned to tell the girl who acted as our maid: *Just say nothing at all; there's no danger for you;* or else; offering herself, propitiatory victim, so that we may escape, her daughter, her mother, her sister: *Just say there's nobody here, say you don't know,* and hanging about, although time is running short, hanging about long enough so that, having got their hands on her, they not busy themselves looking for us.

And so having had her sister and mother leave the house by way of the Upper Road, having, prior to that, crossed that road to put me in a place of safety (so she believed! but perhaps she did not miscalculate after all, since I eluded the trap, escaped capture, though otherwise than she had planned), put me in a place of safety in the house next door—oh, how little time she must have had, to leave me as she did, without explanation or preparation, in the keeping of neighbors concerning whom she knows nothing whatever except that they are neighbors of ours and that I play with their daughter; or perhaps having told herself that these being ordinary people, without any expressed political opinions, they'll be on no one's list and I will spend an undisturbed day in their midst. Until the danger goes away, and we are all back together again, with everything peaceful again. So she believes.

29

On my awakening that morning I recall my mother's gentle touch, I recall her hand gently waking me, not yet aware that this is not going to be an ordinary day; my mother waking me, having me get up, dressing me, and there is already an urgency in her gestures and in her voice telling me over and over again, without my knowing why, without my understanding: *Your name is Jeanne Duval, your name is Jeanne Duval*–a patent untruth, an embarrassment, for Jeanne is my cousin and I do not like taking her name, a lie that, however, I accept as I always accept, unquestioningly, whatever comes to me from her, lovingness, nourishment, attentions, cleaning of scrapes and scratches, bandagings, judgments, prohibitings. *Your name is Jeanne Duval* she says to me and I start calling myself Jeanne Duval despite it being my cousin's name. We are standing side by side in front of the mirror of a wardrobe which would have been between the door and my bed. We are standing very close to each other, it may be that she is doing my braids which bend and are fastened above each ear by plaid taffeta ribbons, and she says to me: *We are going to go over to the Balards'*, and she adds *there is nothing to worry about* and I believe this untruthful voice since it emanates from her who for me is very omniscience and very omnipotence, but at the same time I perceive the inconsistency without telling myself so, without even knowing that I perceive it and that I am burying it away inside me that it revive there more than thirty years afterward, revive now, as I write. And once we have crossed the road it is the same urgency I hear in her voice straining to convince the neighbors, it is the same phrase: *There's no danger for you, there's no danger for you,* a patent lie that satisfies them for no more than an instant, for the time it takes her to turn around, recross the road and then get herself arrested practically in front of my nose. *All I'm asking you to do is keep her here for me, there's no danger for you,* words that register somewhere inside me as plainly false, for if there really weren't anything for any of us to worry about there wouldn't be such insisting, such haste, such a quivering in her usually calm and steady voice straining now to persuade, to enjoin behavior, to become action.

She leaves me and goes away after giving me, probably, a kiss, after saying–ah, what might she have said, exactly? *'Bye? See you in a little while?*–and crosses back to the other side of the road and goes back into our house to repeat to the maid–sixteen years old, just twice my age, two round pink cheeks, skirts with great big flowery patterns on them and gathers with shoulder straps held apart by a horizontal band across the front, and who, the day before, confessed to me in the meadow where the two of us were collecting grass for the rabbits, who confessed to me how horribly embarrassed she was when last night at the circus the educated donkey had designated her as the most amorous person in the whole audience; and I, without understanding, nodded gravely to express my sympathy–, to repeat to the maid: *Just say there's nobody here* and *You aren't in any danger* and walks forth to be

arrested by the three gray-green officers whom I watch
get out of a little car whose color I have forgotten,
whom I see look in the direction being indicated by a
little old woman all in black at whom I am gazing
serenely, even mockingly, through the wide-mesh net
curtain, since I trust her word and since she has never
yet failed me, deceived me, betrayed me, and since she
knows what she is doing and since there isn't anyone
who can outdo her. And while I am thinking: *But
they'll never catch her, she's too smart* (by now I have
grasped, I have accepted the danger), almost delighting
at their stupidity, delighting, after that, in her intelli-
gence and her power over people and events, hands
draw me back, away from the window in order that I
not see my mother set out again accompanied now by
three officers of the SS and above all, I tell myself
today, in order that from outside I not be seen watching
through the glass and possibly about to open the
window with a cry of *Maman!* and especially lest that
call the vindictiveness of the Germans down upon
these quiet folks who above all want to go on minding
their own business. As indeed my mother said before
setting out again: *This doesn't involve you, you are
absolutely in no danger, all you need to do is look after
her for the day.* And who, eager to remain uninvolved,
send me off to get caught elsewhere, send me off down
the road she has just taken, to the school where she is
now. And where, humming to myself as I do every day
as I walk along, I arrive at length to make the sudden
discovery, in the silence and the uniformly appalled
stares which greet me, that perhaps she is not omnip-

otent, that perhaps one mustn't have blind confidence in her under all circumstances, that she may sometimes be in error–since she had promised me that we were in no danger, neither she nor I.

2

So many things have come and gone for me: homes moved into, homes moved out of; studies, a love affair, travels, doubts; another love affair, a living to earn, a marriage, the ocean crossed, two continents that I think of as equally mine, a child brought into the world, a divorce; another love affair . . .

One fine day I made a trip back to the country of my childhood. With me were a man I cared for, and my daughter, a girl with sleek, unruly brown hair, a girl of the very same age I was when I first arrived at Chamberet, provided then with a father and mother, only to lose the father there, definitively, under far from clear circumstances whose recital–whether it be of real or imagined events–offends me, galls me, causes me pain; only to lose my mother there, temporarily, it is true, but a year is a long time when you are only eight and when the future appears to such a degree uncertain . . .

My mother . . . only to lose her and to find her again, fourteen months later, the same in substance and in features though skeleton-thin and her hair cropped short and full of enormous nits which I didn't pay much attention to, being so overcome with joy to have her back again, to have her smile back, the expression of her eyes, the touch of her hand, the feel of her cheek . . . My mother, her face the same and her body the same despite the differences that didn't count for me; and with all that, not the same even if outside it didn't show, or rather potentially not the same, like my uncle, though not in the same way as my uncle who, apparently sound after coming back from Buchenwald, succumbs almost over night the first winter following his return, having contracted a sinus infection which degenerates into septicimia and kills him although he didn't seem to have anything seriously wrong. With my mother it is in a different way that I do not find her the same in the years that ensue, it is in her lack of fighting spirit, her refusal to stand up in connection with the little events of daily life–she who endured the retreat from Auschwitz, on foot and in the snow, in January, across the whole breadth of death-ridden Germany; she who before that had survived through I do not know how many months and how many weeks in the camp in the marshlands, the camp of slow death and of sudden death, Auschwitz-Birkenau whose chimney smokes without ever stopping, whose crematorium burns without ever stopping (and when the gas chamber is out of order, into that crematorium's fires is poured an entire trainload of live children convoyed

from the East, whose screaming goes on all night long);
she who made the dying get back upon their feet in the
make-believe hospital and marched them past the
extermination doctor, in their behalf opting for life that
was unlivable but where one could still hope to be
saved and to return home instead of the certain death
which followed the admission of fatigue–and some of
those sick, gaunt, emaciated women did return from
Auschwitz, some of them told me of the relentless will
to live and to preserve life she had displayed, the
steadfast, the instinctive faith animating her, my
mother, never giving way until now that she is back,
refusing, now that the game has been won, to do battle
once more for her own self and, before the refusal of
self which gradually takes over in her, leaving me, her
would-be champion, to defend an image I have of her
and which she wants nothing more to do with, and to
assume roles that have been hers, adopting them
blindly, even in the evocation I am attempting of the
days she spent in an extermination camp . . .

I have made a trip back to the country of my
childhood so as to share it with those I love right now:
a man and a child, a girl with dark brown hair, full of
life and curiosity, whose presence, paradoxically, pre-
vents me from recapturing the dreamy little girl I was
then, my blond hair done in braids that looped upward
behind my ears. In my passionate refusal to accept the
ugly death of my father, did I really embellish everything connected with the world around me? I remember the garden behind the bent lozenges of its chicken
wire barrier which kept me from getting through but

allowed me to see. I remember the garden, yes, I
remember its box-tree borderings which they doubtless
trimmed and which are growing back unevenly, below
the steps the blue hydrangeas kept a bright color by
means of crumbled up bits of slate, the two symmetrical and strong-smelling thuyas, the first primroses, of
such pale yet intense hues, and the tiger lilies whose
pollen dusts my nose when I go to take a close look at
them. An unusual garden, no; all the same it is there
that I, formerly a city child, came to know the excite-
ment of the first violet and of the first wild strawberry,
there that the marigolds sown by my mother took over
little by little and the strawberry plants she put in one
side proliferated in all directions, spreading over beds
and pathways. This garden where I learn about the
bitter taste of box leaves and the faintly rancid sourness
of a sprig of thuya, this garden where I skip and run
about, obediently keeping clear of the flower-beds,
where I play all by myself atop the narrow wall, with
both hands clinging to the wire to elude my imaginary
pursuer, this garden that has, to one side, a slippery
embankment which I scramble up to get at the white
bushes, fragile hawthorn, sickly sweet syringa, and
another bush with pulpy round berries that collapse to
stickiness between my persistent fingers, this garden
which is so present in my mind, pear-tree in espalier
against one wall, against another the apricot-tree that
bears only one year in two; I suddenly discover,
shocked, that this garden no longer exists anywhere
except in me, who, become an adult, have just come
back for a visit to find the whole place done over in

today's style, with a lawn and a vine or two put in, transforming into a vacation home the hewn granite house where I spent the key years of my life; garden and house which may have been drab, unsightly, or so at least I am told, but where I learned to look at, to listen to, to smell and feel the countryside; garden, house that I am trying to bring back to life today in my search for an abode as distinct from one of those present-day country places that belong on a stage.

Of the rabbit hutch where I once again see my mother, wearing boots and short thick gloves full of cracks and holes, wielding a pitchfork, clearing out the maggotty litter one day when, I suppose, she hadn't found anyone else to attend to the job; of the barn where we kept the supply of firewood that went into our fireplaces, stoves and kitchen range and where we also kept our buckwheat feed, the round grains of buckwheat for the chickens and pigeons and that you scooped out of the bin with a large can that was copper on the outside and like brass inside while the poultry pecked and fluttered and fought between your feet; of the barn, where again I see my mother, still in boots, still wearing gloves, brandishing a big hypodermic syringe and giving injections to the ailing chickens that our neighbor picks up and holds for her one by one: the last to receive treatment is my favorite, white, ruffled, whom I keep watch over and who gets well, the way it ought to because it's my mother who's treating it, and the way all the other chickens do too; of the rabbit hutch and the barn no longer existing as such except in my mind (and in hers perhaps, if she still thinks about them) and that I am eager to show to my daughter, who is the age I was then but born thirty years later, and to the man I am in love with who for his part is perhaps able to imagine, on the basis of his own past, what I am unable to show him because it doesn't exist anymore save in my memory, cherished, nurtured, preserved– because there was something miraculous about the joyfulness of that childhood, glorious in the midst of a world-wide failure, bright in the bitter-cold, rugged heart of the Monédières, exuberant at the height of a period of restrictions and privations–, and of that past there remains in this insipid dwelling nothing but a main building become accessory, exposed beams and dangling planters of geraniums out of place in this Corrèze of heather, ferns and chestnuts, and an anemic lawn trying to hide the courtyard where, when I was little, chickens and pigeons used to peck away, the courtyard which separated our house from the kitchen garden, the courtyard where all our itineraries converged. It was in the courtyard I played with the faucet despite my mother having forbidden it. Water flows from a brass tap into a rectangular stone tub outside the kitchen window. I, playing in the garden, I have solemnly promised not to touch it either today or in any of the days to come. But here is the neighbors' boy Michel, two years older than I and the one I am getting ready to marry once I am eight, wearing by way of a bridal veil one of the wide-mesh net curtains full of all sorts of motifs which hang in our and in everybody else's windows; here's Michel who, guessing my most secret desires, incites me to turn on the forbidden faucet, pledging not to tell. A pledge no sooner made than broken, and he has me in his power, helpless: *I'll say you turned on the water,* a piece of blackmail that achieves its purpose in the groundless terror it inspires in me (groundless terror, for after all what have I to fear from going myself to tell my mother that I have disobeyed her?), and in return for silence he asks nothing except, probably, the fun of seeing my panic and listening to my supplications.

The courtyard through which my mother will cross, coming up from the garage by the tree-lined path, after a long series of calls, at all hours, in all kinds of weather; and whose shining black boots I wait to see against the green of the meadow, and the large, lustreless black satchel with its big white metal clasp standing out against the pebble-grained leather. During this period my mother is all in black, coat, satchel, boots, or all in white, white smock worn over her clothes which always smell a little of ether, for me no longer dissociable from her own odor; and overfloating all that black, or all that white, her blondness, her gentleness, her smile when she catches sight of me. And afterwards when I come back to this Chamberet in the fall of 1945 and we reinstall ourselves in our house, without my mother, nobody knowing where she is or when she will return (for *whether* she will return is something we do not dare to say), I play in this courtyard near the wooden gate that separates it from the meadow and I make myself cry at will by summoning up thoughts of shining black boots and the large, lustreless pebble-grained satchel coming up the steep path, so strongly visible against the background of green grass and against the carpet of needles fallen from the fir-trees in certain spots.

Also in this courtyard, another one of her itineraries, older: for it was before my father's death that Maman used to move gaily back and forth between the kitchen and the vegetable garden she would work in and where I would be with her, sowing and planting just as I saw her do and beholding, O miracle! the sprouting and then the growth of a couple of green peas, a carrot, a lettuce in the one square yard which had been allotted to me in order that I too cause seed to fructify and bring life forth from the soil. A place where the maid also came and went, not the sixteen-year-old but the other, for that too was before: as ancient, as little, as shriveled up as could be, dressed in black and turned into a figure eight by the apron-string tightly tied around her tiny waist and, a white line, denoting the meeting place of the two loops of the figure eight her shape describes; hair in a wee little knot on the top of her head, *Tiou, tiou* she calls, or else *Chick, chick, chick* and there is a rush and a flurry all around us, the boldest of the hens perching and cackling on the tin that once contained preserves and is now three-quarters full of little grains, round and dark in color, which beneath the vigorous beaks of the gallinaceans will be transformed into proteins and will feed us in our turn; initially to my great indignation, expressed in a refusal to partake of the flesh of creatures we saw being born, tumble out of the egg, take refuge under the protecting wings of the brood-hen, then walk, then find their sustenance all by themselves, then disappear into the throng as little by little they take on size and feathers; after that to my profound indifference, back of which lay my gluttony.

This courtyard is the place where during this period I often play with Michel of the runny nose, who takes pleasure in terrorizing me by threatening to go and tell my mother that I have fiddled about with the water. Believing him, I weep and beg him to keep quiet. He agrees, magnanimous. I thank him. Then he starts again, every day, several times a day. Be that as it may, we are to get married as soon as I am eight years old, and by way of a wedding veil I shall wear one of the curtains hanging in the ground floor windows. Instead of which, I do not know why, my mother gets herself arrested and I come within an ace of witnessing, through these same curtains which also adorn the windows of our neighbors' house, the sight of my mother leaving between a pair of German officers and getting into the little car I saw stop in front of our house, thinking to myself: *But they'll never catch her, she's much too smart,* and gloating . . . but not for long.

3

And when I come to this point in what I have been saying I am at an end, having reached the bottom of myself. Still wishing to go on, I manage it by doing so outside of myself, that is, by relating what I have experienced through another person rather than directly, by relating things she told of when later on she returned, told over the course of days and over the course of years, things which I grew up on for a long time, as a child, as an adolescent, and that I listened to without a word, evening after evening, then one evening out of two, then one out of three, then one evening a week, one a month, and finally no longer, but which remain inside me, buried in my depths, something hardened, some stone-like cyst, some node, undetermined in character but persisting, malignant.

When she found herself in the schoolroom, the middle grades classroom, the room where Madame

Nair taught, whose husband, also in the Resistance, was to be killed at the Liberation by the new allies of the collaborator who had informed against my mother (but that is some time away, it won't happen until a few months later), when she found herself in the classroom, with her she had, in her handbag, all the papers, all the falsified identity papers of her family: her sister's, her mother's, who were probably still waiting for her on the Upper Road and who, I imagine, must then have had at last to admit to themselves—exchanging what words, what looks?—that she was not going to join them and that consequently. . . ; must then have had at last to decide to stop waiting for her and to fall back to the place chosen for the second rendezvous—I can only imagine, for I never could take it upon myself to ask, never dared to confront the account I would hear of their emotions, I never was able to bring myself to disclose to them what I felt, because it is unbearable. And so there in her handbag, along with her own, she had the falsified papers of those two women, her mother, her sister, of whose existence the Germans apparently did not know, having, so far, questioned her only about *the child*, me, whose sex remained unspecified and whose presence she was denying—*The child has left, it isn't here anymore*—while at that very moment I was cheerily entering the schoolhouse, walking into the room just across the hall where the children from both classes were gathered, running straight into their silence, their stares—and to this day I still cannot tolerate being stared at or having someone stand there in front of me and keep obstinately still. And, I don't know quite how, between badgerings, between denials, she managed to fish those papers out of her bag and to slip them behind her into the desk she was leaning back against (those papers being found there later, after her departure towards the place where *Arbeit macht frei*), for others, for her loved ones instinctively hitting on the right gesture, the saving words, at the same time not bothering about herself, naively believing that in her dealings with History she disposed of the same immunity she assumed as a physician with regard to the risks of catching a patient's disease.

She slipped those papers into the desk behind her back–her hand brings them from her handbag where it has just occurred to her that they are, or did it cross her mind on the way here, while covering that half-mile from our house to the town hall, and what indeed were her thoughts on the way? The moment when time is at a halt, the moment when the body tenses and when the mind empties, when the whole of you empties out in order to meet the oncoming catastrophe: *This time it's for me.* And with that, I imagine, the same reflex: *Let's not get excited* and the reflex to protect her dear ones. Once, long after the period I am telling about here, she and I were in a car driving in the Midi, and suddenly the car skids, spins all the way around, and stops crosswise in the middle of the pavement; and she, who is at the wheel, imperturbable: *Let's not get excited.* Later I asked her–I was perhaps fifteen–just who actually she had been talking to. *I? Why, did I say that?* and she recalled for me what the surgeon she had studied

47

under used to say in delicate situations: *Let's not get excited.* That April morning, seated beside or between gray-green officers in the car that took her away, I imagine that once the initial shock was past, the moment of disbelief got beyond, the *This time it's for me* surmounted, she must have likewise urged herself to be calm and told herself to concentrate upon saving her family, buttressing herself with this or that concrete detail–the falsfied papers, their not knowing whether the child was a boy or a girl–in order to recover her calm, surmount her confusion and in the meantime save her dear ones. I imagine that, for that is how I function in the face of those everyday catastrophes which, though not having anything to do with History, are just as distressing sometimes, connected as they may be with the fear of death or irreparable injury. I imagine . . . And I think too that she did not realize where she was heading, and that that helped her; I also think that never, in the conversations which at night I overheard her having with my uncle, who also spoke without any awareness of his coming fate, did the word *deportation* give rise in them to the idea of that systematic and deliberate extermination they were both going to have to affront, because in the world governed by reason and where man was the measure of all things, the world they had both been brought up in, the notion of death camps was inconceivable.

And now, the telltale papers temporarily eliminated both from her handbag and from her life, silence preserved regarding the actual sex of the child and its presence obstinately denied (my trajectory having, without her realizing it, brought us to within a hairs-breadth of meeting, following an elliptical movement which from a collision course veers away just as immutably as a moment ago it was approaching, this bearing off in a different direction having saved her life as well as mine, for upon arrival at Auschwitz, where she did not yet know she was bound, a child accompanying a woman condemned her to death as certainly as a leprosy or an infirmity; since upon arrival at Auschwitz, to which unbeknownst to her every instant was bringing her nearer, a woman with her child did not even penetrate into the camp, but were both directed by soldiers toward trucks which carried them straight to the gas chamber), she in her turn leaves the school, all blondness and dignity, still protected (not for much longer, but this too she does not yet know) by the fact she is a woman, by the fact she is a doctor, by her status, lost only recently, of a British subject. And her arrest once reported, a member of the family, in an effort to save her, will seek in vain to obtain the intervention of the embassy of the country with which she identified her childhood, her youth, but whose pomps and satisfactions she gladly renounced when she married my father so as to become a citizen of the country she naively believed to be that *mère des arts, des armes et des lois* celebrated in Du Bellay. But at this point there is nothing left of all that but the pistols hanging from the belts of the puzzled and woebegone men who as representatives of a so-called law power-less to defend those under its jurisdiction hold her at the gendarmerie in Treignac, where she spends, I know not under what conditions nor with what thoughts, her first night of captivity. After that one there are around three hundred ninety-five more to come.

From Treignac they take her to Limoges, where she embroiders a pink batiste apron for me, a simple rectangle done into symmetrical pleats held by a band at the top. Along the edge of the hem, which is abnormally wide, measuring a good third of the entire height, she stitched in white thread the words: *I am thinking of you, Maman.* It is intended for my birthday, which falls in the last week of that month of April when she was arrested, and I don't recall just when the present reaches me but it seems to me that it is much later, towards the time school starts in the fall, when there are no more invaders in our village and we are all back there–all, that is, except her of whom we are utterly without word, who is perhaps dead although we don't speak of it, and whose fate I continue to negotiate with the Almighty newly entered into my life and which has now taken a name: the God of the Catholics, discovered by me during these same days I am talking about, probably the selfsame ones she is spending at work on the apron and charming or outwitting some-body into getting it out and getting it delivered–where? when?–, her behavior affirming her underlying confi-dence, that perfectly irrational faith which throughout the long German winter gives her the strength to induce those half-dead women to get up from their pallets and parade in front of the German doctor to avoid being selected for killing–and she does in fact save a few, they are a drop in the bucket, yes, but they are a few women saved from the enterprise of wholesale destruction, a few real persons who come back and who declare twenty years afterward: *You saved my life. She saved my life.* When we are all back, that is, all except her and except my uncle, her sister's husband of whom we have also had no news, of whom we don't speak either, of whom I shall have little more than a glimpse, since he dies shortly after reaching home.

Limoges, that is where she is, in the Haute-Vienne, whereas I am at Faux-la-Montagne in the Creuse. For me it is the time when I discover true Frenchmen: though, to be sure, I am not able to define just what it is, I do note the difference, very subjectively perceived, between myself and them. True Frenchmen: those that are not somewhat Jewish, those who are not a little bit Russian or Polish, those who speak but one tongue which is their own, those who are attached to the soil and to its products, whether modest–the dandelions that I learn to eat in a salad with little bits of fried bacon on top–, or, a little later, in the Gers, more sumptuous: the vineyards, the wine upon an estate whose epicenter is a castle, the secularized one-time residence of the Bishops of Auch where the ancient kitchen has a Cistercian vault and the garden a magnolia-tree. This is the time when I put down roots in France, because that richness and that diversity, that feast for my eyes, for my nose, for my taste-buds, is all I have left. The kindness of others is not enough.

The first night she is away, locked in the Treignac gendarmerie, I am at a loss. I cannot indeed imagine where she is, what she is doing while I for my part, in the barn, in utter darkness, am listening for hours on end to the nibbling of the mice and the hooting of the owl, huddled up in a lawn chair opposite my aunt and my grandmother. Before daybreak my aunt goes off, at dawn it's I who set forth; the familial diaspora has begun. As for my grandmother, she will go into hiding for months and months in an attic belonging to a woman she barely knows and whom my mother saw maybe once or twice about a lingering cold or cramps in the legs; an uneducated woman we wouldn't have invited to our house or to tea or to join us for music on Sunday afternoon, to play on our out-of-tune dark rosewood upright piano, by the warmth of the fire burning in the imitation marble fireplace with its great brass-framed rectangular mirror over the mantelpiece; whom we wouldn't have invited to come to share some cake made from potato-flour according to the recipes my mother is so proud of and that she has pasted into a copybook where she records her progress in the adventure of cooking and in improvisations during this period of wartime rationing and shortages. (At Auschwitz, in later months, they will call that *organizing*; more precisely, for the men and women whose job is to sort the heaps of belongings and commodities taken from the deportees upon their arrival in the camp, to organize will be to salvage a few essential articles, a slice of bread, a chip of soap, a piece of underwear, and to smuggle them, either as a gift or in exchange for something else, into the camp where these fabulous objects represent luxury, the longed for, survival.)

And that woman without education and whom one wouldn't have had over for music on a Sunday afternoon in winter-time, unwed mother with a questionable past in the city, an overblown blonde with overly large eyes and overly full lips, turns up during broad daylight and without further ado takes my grandmother by the hand and leads her home to her house, smack in the center of the village, opens a trap door, has her climb up into her attic, almost touching the tower of the village church. In the attic she fixes a bed for her, brings food to her, takes away the water she has used to wash in, sometimes comes up for a chat; in a word, saves her, physically and mentally, and does it without fanfare, without vainglory, naturally, as a matter of course, as if she'd done nothing else all her life, as if heroism were everyday stuff with her. I think of my grandmother, come from a Russian Jewish middle-class family, a woman who had lived in several European capitals, who had had servants, jewels, furs, an English governess for her three daughters, who had, over the course of the years, conversed alternately in Russian, in Polish, in English, who speaks French to be sure, but with an accent and mistakes that I with my eight-year-old's asperity disapprove of, and who holes up for months in a dark and airless attic, during daytime reduced to complete immobility, for nobody must be allowed to suspect her presence; after nightfall walking back and forth to take the stiffness out of her limbs, talking with her hostess who can then, her son once in bed and asleep (he is my age and knows nothing about the stranger who, however, despite herself and merely by dint of being there, places his life at risk), once there is no likelihood of a visit from any of the neighbors, who can then mount the ladder and arrive through the trap door with the pittance and warming words of sympathy. What an odd friendship develops between these two women, so different through age, through social background, through their outlook and prejudices and their past experience, one of whom, her work once finished for the day, comes up the ladder, every day for five months, and settles down for a conversation with the other she has kept imprisoned for the purpose of saving her, for her accent would get her arrested anywhere; jailer and pedagogue too, for at the end of five months my grandmother has almost no more accent and when she finally comes down out of there, and when I finally find her again some time after the Liberation, she is speaking French just about fluently, she has become accustomed to the language and to those who speak it and become at home with them, having then and, like me, for the first time been in steady and immediate contact with people who are French and nothing else. I think that for my grandmother as for me a sense of belonging was achieved through the people and the things of a village—in my case through sensorial discoveries, wonderful discoveries of sight, of smell, of taste, which coincided with a profound feeling of inner destitution; for her, I imagine, through the conversations she had with an interlocutress whose words brought her the revelation of a humble and rural everyday life of which she had been in completest ignorance. What are my grandmother's thoughts as the clock in the church-tower close by tolls the passing hours while she lies stretched out upon her straw mattress, without being able to read, without being able to move about, unable even to cough or sneeze, for every sound can be heard through those warped, loosely joined planks that serve as a floor and which constitute the ceiling of the room below. At one point she cannot repress a sneeze. It's the cat, her mindful jailer explains to the neighbor who happens to have just dropped in for a visit. Does the neighbor believe her? Nothing ensues. The neighbor may have been taken in; if not, then it's that she wishes us no ill.

My mother is in Limoges, I am at Faux-la-Montagne, probably dazed, not altogether there, though unaware of my state. It is only today that I know enough to recognize that kind of stupor, that anaesthesia, that putting on hold of everything in me capable of feeling and therefore of suffering as so many signs of break-down, indissociable from an effort to regain possession of myself that enables me to keep going, to bear up, to skip rope, to go to school. As I was saying just now, I deaden within myself everything which would be susceptible of feeling and of suffering. Simulta-neously—as, after all, one must look somewhere for nourishment—my sight, my sense of smell, of taste become keener. While I have become incapable of shedding tears or of telling myself I am in pain, instead I look, I listen, I inhale, I gather everything in. Because were I willing to dwell upon my loss—the sudden, unexpected, unforeseeable disappearance of her who is everything to me (a disappearance which repeats and

consequently drives further home the sudden, unexpected, unforeseeable disappearance, one fine Novem-
ber morning, of my father, and in his case it was forever
and I never saw him again except dead and ghastly
white and on one side of his face because I don't quite
know how the other side was and I have always refused
to imagine, going so far as to faint because of a drop of
blood seeping from a cut fingertip or which might
redden my toothbrush while brushing my teeth)–,
because if I consented to dwell upon this absence I
might not have the strength to go on living and neither
do I have the strength to give up life: in the park it was
that *She yes but not me,* when we, my aunt, my
grandmother and I were trying to make ourselves one
with the yew-trees and invisible. Just as, so as to go on
living, I take refuge in the tart taste, a new taste for me,
of dandelions and bacon, I also take refuge, so as to
continue to live without suffering, in the newness of
the odors and the newness of the customs hereabouts.
There is for instance the moldy odor of cold stone in
the passageway leading to the courtyard where I skip
rope, indissociable from the sadness that accompanies
the oncoming of night, odor of stone, of moldiness and
of urine, risen from the grayness which absorbs all
light, drains all color. In days past, in my own village,
I used to go for the milk at this same hour. Andrée
Balard, my neighbor, my best friend, she and I would
walk down from the village. The paved road seemed
tremendously wide, bordered on both sides by hedges
of flowerless hawthorn bushes and blackthorns without fruit. Together we would go down the hill, carrying

our milk-cans, and head for the farm where the cows had just been milked. In autumn, in winter, when we started out the sun would be setting, and to the left, against the flushed sky, stood out the dark shape of the hedge and the tall silhouettes of occasional beeches growing in its midst. When we reached La Malatie at the intersection of two roads and at the very point where the ground stopped sloping down and began to slope upward, in winter, in autumn the fire would be going in the big fireplace flanked on either side by chests where they had us seat ourselves, Andrée and I, while waiting for the return of the daughter-in-law who did the milking. Logs would be burning in the fireplace and the smell of the smoke would combine with the aroma of the cabbage soup simmering there in a soot-covered cast-iron pot sometimes placed on a tripod or else, when the fire was going strong, hung from a hook ending in three metal loops, the hook hanging from a pot-hanger itself hooked to a chain, and all that in order to regulate the amount of heat reaching the pot so that its contents could cook without burning. Upon the long rectangular table to our right soup bowls of white crockery with a blue pattern were set out and waiting, full of bread cut up in small pieces. And when the daughter-in-law was late, the mistress of the house brought the soup to the table and put a ladleful into each bowl, on top of the bits of bread whose keen odor blended pleasantly with that of the cabbage and that of the woodsmoke, and then placed the lid back on each bowl so that the bread would steep and swell, and everything would keep hot. Afterwards when we walked back home still smelling that good smell and carrying our halfway filled milk-cans, the sky would be dark and the silhouettes of the hedgerows and trees would have become black. Andrée Balard used to swing her milk-can in a circle, very fast and without losing a drop; while I regretted not knowing how or not daring to do it, afraid of spilling. Each went home to her house, cheeks and hands red from the cold, eyes saturated with bright colors and light, nose filled with good odors. Now on the contrary the evenings are gray, everything smells of sadness and loneliness, and the walls of the courtyard and of the house are all there is in the way of a horizon. I wouldn't yet use the word common to describe my new playmates but that is what I feel about them as, skipping rope, I gaze at them and realize little by little, amidst the odor of mold, of urine and of cold stone, that I am not the same as they.

Or again the odor of church, where I go every Sunday morning to mass, all dressed up in my freshly laundered new Sunday dress–new because it doesn't belong to me and because it was part of the hastily constituted outfit (two pairs of underpants, two undershirts, three pairs of socks, three handkerchiefs, one dress, and how were these people able to come up with all that from one moment to the next in the middle of a war?) that I found in the chest of drawers at the head of the new bed awaiting me when I arrived in Faux-la-Montagne at the end of a day full of sunshine and green grass. It had been a real country outing organized by four young people, two couples on bikes, out enjoying themselves on a lovely day in early spring; and who would find anything amiss about their having a child with them, straddling the bar, which hurts, but I don't dare complain any more than a little later at table I dare say anything when the food is served to everybody but me and, inadvertently forgotten, I sit silently watching the grown-ups eat, hoping that someone will finally notice that I am hungry. New also because I have never had a Sunday dress, Sunday socks, Sunday shoes and because the latter, neat and clean and painful when I have them on, convince me of the day's solemnity or rather of the morning's, as does the big white ribbon tied in my hair pulled good and tight to go to mass. At church it is a jumble of discoveries: the odor of incense, the Ave Maria, and that the men are above while the women and children are down below. I go to mass every Sunday, I say my prayers–I don't mind doing it at all: has any of that anything really to do with me? Indeed, I believe that in this period I also learned about the relativity and the flexibility of manners and customs. A month of this and I find out that I am to go somewhere else. I am taken in a bus in the direction of Limoges, where my mother is in the hospital. And to get closer to my mother, although I know I'll not see her because she is in prison in the hospital, fills me with emotion and joy–and it is only today, as I write this, that it occurs to me to question this idea of a hospital.

Of Limoges, where we wander about for a time, I have an impression of grayness and height. After a lot of walking this way and that way we wind up inside the central post office. There I come upon my aunt, who bursts into tears at seeing me, and inwardly I am terribly angry at her for not knowing how to contain her feelings. I do not yet know that her husband, my uncle, was arrested yesterday or the day before while trying to cross into Spain on his way to join the Free French in London. Neither do I know—or if at the time I glimpsed the truth I hid it away somewhere because it was too frightening to think about—that I too came near to being caught in Chamberet last month and that but for the sang-froid and the impromptu heroism of several people, the chances were that I would be turning into a little pile of ashes in a partially drained swamp on the confines of Germany and Poland.

For it is to Auschwitz my mother goes away: Treignac, Limoges, Drancy, Auschwitz, loaded, like all the others, into one of those freight cars forming the long, windowless, sealed trains which coming from East and West traverse the whole of a Germany that does not want to see them, that does not want to hear the cries that sometimes come from them, that never asks itself questions about those strings of freight cars standing overnight along the platforms, freight cars giving out periodic moans and screams. To Auschwitz my mother goes, in slow stages, inexorably, once the process has been set in motion—through the informing of a man she had never done any harm to but who could not tolerate sharing his clientele and who had seized the occasion, when the Germans came through, to be rid of her, deliberately, with a word pronounced in the privacy of his office. *There aren't any Jews here,* the town clerk had told the German officer who had asked for a list of them. *One moment,* the mayor had said and he had requested the German officer to step into his office, and upon reappearing from there that officer had gone straight to our house where I saw him arrive as I peered through the curtains in the neighboring house, thinking: *But they'll never catch her, she's much too smart.*

To Auschwitz where they are ordered down onto the ramp after how many days, how many nights penned in railroad cars where twice as many human beings were forced into the space animals would have required; to Auschwitz after how many nights, how many days without drinking and without eating, without pissing, without shitting. There at Auschwitz are the green-gray soldiers, there is a road, there is a line of waiting trucks. *If you are tired,* say the soldiers, *climb aboard one of the trucks.* It must be that she has begun to understand how the thing works; or it is simply that the contrast is too great between this solicitude and the brutality, the cruelty of that first stage in the program of systematic degradation, the journey in the freight cars where human beings, so packed together they cannot move, have to stand day after day, night after night. It must be that at this point, for her, the limits of the believable suddenly give way. Or else her self-preservation instinct starts to guide her, though only a short while ago it did not prevent her from falling victim to her sense of invulnerability–unless, yet again, as will a lark or the female of some species of bird whose name eludes me, she returned–perhaps voluntarily? perhaps unconsciously?–in order that her trace be picked up and the hunters diverted away from her progeniture. And from her sister. And mother. Whatever the reason, she declines the offer of departure by truck, and in doing so preserves her life. For while she along with a great many others proceeds on foot down the road leading to the gateway with its sardonic inscription assuring *Freedom through work*, the trucks drive off, filled with women, children, elderly persons, perhaps invalids, all those that is who after those long nights and those long days standing in the freight cars admit their weariness. Well, those trucks do not even enter the camp. Straight to the gas chamber they go, where under the color of hygiene those unclothed people are crowded into vast shower rooms where instead of water it is poisonous gas that issues from the shower heads. Have I seen, have I read of, have I dreamt of those clusters of naked bodies clambering up pipes towards the ceiling, clutching whatever on the wall provides a hand-hold, straining in the direction of illusory windows, sealed transoms through which only light passes, naked hosts frozen still, agglutinated. For those corpses, the crematorium. More fortunate, those victims, than the ones–an entire trainful of living children–that are burned without first being gassed when toward the end they run out of gas, and whose screaming fills the whole of a night that makes stand on end the hair growing back on the lately shaved heads of those who however by now must be inured to horror. An entire train filled with children brought from the East, not gassed first but burnt, as is, such as they arrive. Later on in the course of her talking during that unending series of evenings, sometimes her voice breaks, a lone tear wells up in each of her eyes, and I, ten years old, eleven, twelve, I do not stir, I listen, I am initiated into the secrets of modern times and of History, and I wait in the expectation that she will write, that she will bear witness and make her protest known. But she does not, and so it is I who out of the stories she told am weaving her protest, in her behalf and in her name, twenty years, thirty years afterward, I now being a good deal older than she was at the time, and my own daughter having just reached the age I was then. A generation later.

Our paths diverged, the paths of a child and its mother suddenly, forcibly separated, and yet we underwent a simultaneous experience, our experience of the war. Hers included famine, cold, sickness, physical exhaustion, mental harassment; but also–because her sense of personal dignity and of intrinsic human worth was stronger than the concerted attempt to degrade the human person that she together with millions of others was subjected to–it included struggle, it included the affirmation of the supremacy of human values, humanistic values, over the forces of evil, of destruction, of extermination. It would be summer when she arrives at Auschwitz and, because she is a doctor, she escapes the forced marches, the toil with pick and shovel, the work connected with the draining of the swamp. But she does not escape the want, the dysentery, she too is reduced to skin and bones, the chimney is there for her too, and the ever present smoke, and the selections for the gas chamber to which those women around her are driven in swarms; she does not escape the roll-calls, standing out of doors at attention for hours, no matter what the weather, and as time passes those roll-calls are conducted under the rain, in mud, while it snows, in the wind, in the cold, nor later does she escape the terrible retreat across the whole of Germany, on foot and in the snow and in the depths of winter.

She who a short time before, upon the death of my father, had thought she had been through the worst, taking over his practice from one day to the next and without having had time to prepare herself, starting at once to go out on house calls throughout the country-side before she was really a capable driver, and the car being the very one in which he had been first struck unconscious and then drowned, she whose beginnings as a country doctor came in a period of gasoline shortage and during winter time when roads are treach-erous, she who became inventive, driving with two wheels on the snow-covered shoulder so as to keep the other two on the slippery pavement, descending any kind of hill in neutral to save on fuel, she who more than once had to hunt at dawn for her car buried under the snow that had fallen during a night spent delivering or waiting to deliver a baby, or, again, been unable to find the road to the farm after having done several kilometers at night in the snow and fog on her way to an emergency; she who, talking about it today, says that the nails were the most awful part, *I'd sit down by the side of the road wringing my hands until someone came along who could change the tire for me;* she whom in those days, in the midst of bereavement, in the midst of the difficulties of taking over a clientele scattered all over the highlands, in the midst of anxieties about the future that the war was preparing, I never saw otherwise than cheerful when we met at home at the end of the day, cheerful and sweet and always there; she who wore a smile on the morning which was to be the morning of her arrest, when she came in to wake me up early: *Claude, wake up,* I still hear her voice, soft as ever; and again: *Claude, wake up,* and her luminous, smiling face which transformed this rude awakening, gently transformed it into something somehow normal, and the incomprehensible words coming from her lips: *Your name is Jeanne Duval, your name is Jeanne Duval* (she had also said: *And I will come back to get you . . .*)—it is she who today is experiencing the cold horror of the concentration camp world, with its implacable logic bearing no relation to the real and daily conditions in that world, and who then, a little later, in the worst of the German winter, will participate in the terrible retreat, on foot and in the snow, the terrible retreat from Auschwitz.

At present she is working in the Birkenau hospital, wearing a smock that she must keep clean and white though she has neither soap nor bleach to wash it. Her formerly long blond hair has been cropped short and it is infested now with vermin and lice. Sweet and full was the face I remember, it has become sunken now, the pink cheeks to which I would press mine have become slack and sallow; the soft hands that were so skilled at bandaging my scratches, at caressing my arms, at untangling and braiding my hair, are now rough and chapped; her entire body has faded, of it there is literally nothing left but the skin on the bones thanks to denutrition, dysentery and, later, the cold when the temperature falls far below freezing. Nevertheless her brown eyes have retained their luminous quality, and she still has her smile, and by her eyes and her smile I have no trouble recognizing her when she returns, despite the forty-five pounds she has lost. And she has retained that belief, that faith in human beings which is stronger than the constant spectacle of men devoted to destroying, that faith in human beings that impels her, there in the extermination camp, to treat the sick, to try to prolong life, be it only for a little. As she has no medicines at her disposal, she cares for her patients by having them lie down and rest, by listening and giving them her attention, by replying. But with the endless threat of a weeding out of those to be fed into the ovens, she saves the dying by making them get up from their beds and leave the hospital so as not to be there when the Aryan doctor arrives, clad in his gray-green uniform, in his gleaming black boots. Here it is he who decides between life and death: *Get up, there's to be a selection soon; go somewhere now, you can return here afterward.* Or by forcing the paralytic to cut a swanking figure before him: *Chin up, chest out, march, you must march, you have got to do it.* And the ambulatory cadaver rises upon its purulent, flopping legs, and walks, *marches*, impassively scrutinized by the exterminator-physician. This time she is saved. Until when? Not long ago it was *Claude, wake up . . . up you get, my little Claude,* so now in this place she saves the lives of a few women, not by the accuracy of her diagnoses, which must nonetheless be faultless in accordance with the insane logic of the death-camp hospital but which is pointless since there are no more medicines with which to attempt a cure than there is soap to keep a smock clean—but by her stubborn insistence upon foiling the exterminatory system within which any vacillation, any mistake is fatal: *Arise, do you hear me? Arise, and walk, walk out of here. Get up, get off the block, go back to the camp, you can return here afterward . . .* That is how by dint of stubbornness she saves herself throughout the retreat from Auschwitz at the end of January, across snow-covered Poland and Germany, on foot, part of that herd of men, that herd of women, so many walking dead, in rags, long since reduced to the last extremity by malnutrition and mistreatment. Certain ones survive, including her, who keep themselves from sinking down by the wayside where soldiers automatically dispatch those who do. Certain ones, among them somebody I have known, manage to get away by rolling down the slope at the edge of the road, burrowing into the snow, blending with it, avoiding the bursts fired after them, then, the column having moved away, heading back in the other direction towards the Polish plain and the oncoming Russian troops who, according to rumor, are no longer very far away and before whom the Nazis are fleeing, having at the last moment abandoned the idea of blowing up Auschwitz, and who are dragging along with them the wretched crowd of those who had deemed best, persuant to death-camp

logic, not to remain behind at the camp and wait but to
take to the road, opting for the more difficult course
but convinced that it alone held out, perhaps, some
chance of safety. Perhaps. For the lengthening column
leaves a trail of corpses behind it; and of all those
women who had thought the wiser thing was to follow
their butchers across the Germany so lovable and
loving in song, only a fraction reach the gates of
Ravensbruck, already filled, from where they are sent
farther on, and yet farther on, to a camp that strikes
them as a benign place although they continue to die
there of hunger, of cold and of dysentery, but benign
because it possesses neither gas chamber nor crematorium, benign because there is no longer that greasy
smoke with the characteristic stench when the wind is
blowing in their direction, benign because they are no
longer likely to have to hear the screams of an entire
trainload of children thrown alive into the flames,
benign because there is no further danger of seeing
their daughter, their mother, their sister, their only
friend set off for the shower room where gas comes
from the sprinklers overhead... Once, the time of
slow death or violent death by now well in the past,
and well after the time, following her return, of repet-
itive, obsessive talk, a litany that would graft itself
upon all other speech and associate itself with any
other image, liberating and also evidence of the hurt
sustained; once, the time having come when she no
longer spoke of the death camps, having succeeded in
starting a new life for herself and in bringing another
child into the world, once, at least thirty years after the

event, she told me about one of those women she had
not been able to save, not been able to induce or force
to get up on her feet in front of the doctor who picked
you for death; or who had tottered and fallen in front of
him, whatever. Upon that day, at least thirty years
afterward, she wept as she told about that woman she
had been unable to save from the gas and whose
daughter, a former concentration camp prisoner too,
she had just unexpectedly run into. She wept because
that daughter, today a woman of mature years, did not
know under what hideous conditions her mother had
perished, and because she herself did know, had seen
her body, mutilated, disfigured, a horror, before it
became a corpse in the showers. She wept because she
did not have the courage to tell the truth to that
person's daughter, and had preferred to leave her in the
belief it had been death from breakdown, from disease
rather than to have to tell her: *They gassed your
mother, they burned her.* But to me she did speak: *If
you had seen the state that woman was in. . .* and tears
rushed from her eyes, her voice broke.

While she did indeed come through, she bears and
will always bear the inner scars of those thirteen
months, a brand more indelible still than the one that
mars her forearm, the tattooed registration number in
blue ink she has never wanted to have removed. Once
home and safe and sound, she refused to forget, as
well-wishers urged her to do. But I have never been able
to find out why she has always refused to tell anyone
about it except us, her kin, whom she told every day.

4

Everything I have just evoked—the terrible retreat from
Auschwitz, on foot across snow-covered Germany, on
foot from its most easterly point, its southeast corner
where it touches Poland, on foot across the whole of
what has since become the Democratic Republic, then
across all of what has become the Federal Republic;
and as it advances westward the miserable column also
moves north, lengthening its journey—all of that tran-
spires at the end of January in the very depths of the
continental winter, on foot and in rags in the deep
snow, on foot and without food in the knee-deep snow.
Through that landscape of whiteness, of silence, whiteness of the earth, whiteness of the sky, for the stillness-
breeding, all-effacing snow continues to fall, the
macabre column, the incredible column trudges slowly
on. But unlike the ones in our childhood nightmares,
these skeletons are not dancing, these skeletons are not

making merry. Painfully, gasping, they drag their rag-bound feet through the clinging snow, each step demanding an appalling effort. But they have no choice, for if they fall, a single shot or a burst from an automatic weapon will nail them to the ground, sprawled bodies slowly disappearing beneath the snow, forms growing ever more imprecise, ripples on the landscape which for a while may give pause to those who are pursuing their march, anonymous monuments gradually levelled by the snow and upon which, by and by, no gaze comes to rest anymore. Thus do human lives pass away.

Late in January of that year I for my part regained my Corrèze, my adopted home, returned to my house, the only house, the only part of the country I can call mine. One lovely day full of the glorious light of late summer and before the beginning of the vine-harvest I did not get to see even though all the work being done by the men around me pointed toward that great moment, one lovely day near the end of the summer my aunt came to fetch me at the gray and ochre chateau, at the chateau whose discreet splendor derives from its proportions, from its ageless stone, from the sweep of its carriage-drive, from its bastion-like central position towards which converge the vineyards its inhabitants depend upon for their livelihood, vineyards laid out in winding rows following the contours of the hilly land, a mottling of green upon the bare ochre, the rose-pink ochre of the earth. At the center, then, there's the chateau, once the residence of the Bishop of Auch, a building in the shape of an *L* against which a church abuts, transforming the *L* into a *U*. From the days of its splendor there remain a facade, ironwork, two staircases which in my opinion are admirable, the Cistercian vault of the former kitchen that is only used as a storeroom now, a bridge that may have been a drawbridge once but which centuries of steady use have left anchored to the masonry spanning the moat, a rounded granite arch, a now dormant bridge lying on shoulders of granite overspread by patches of tiny, intensely pink flowers, wild growth sumptuous in its color which tells both of the southern latitude and of the relatively abandoned state of the old episcopal palace. Of its former splendor there remain the building's proportions, the design of the garden, outlined by boxwood, invaded by tall grass; and there are the magnolias, with their shiny leaves and incredible flowers, huge, creamy flowers which open wider and wider and reveal petals that are opaque, veined, ivory-like, into which I dare not reach my fingers as I am simply dying to do, and whose scent perfumes the air, and which present to me luxuriance, sumptuousness and the exotic all in one. I am well treated in this chateau, surrounded by friendly people. Living here I discover an abundance of rich colors and of golden light, I am free to move about and play as I like both inside the chateau and out, I can choose from among all sorts of places to play in and all sorts of things to play with—a whole storeroom with real wooden crates and real shelves for playing grocery, big blocks of real modeling clay cut right out of the ground with a knife at a spot where a rivulet softens the soil and makes the operation possible; an abundance also of odors, of tastes, of tactile sensations, of objects to behold: sun-ripened figs, warm, juicy, sweet, full of little seeds that crack between my teeth, the so tasty skin of those figs finally–great surprise!–having an irritating effect and making my lips puff up; tart red wine at table, at every meal, my glass of it diluted with water, but which, between meals, I go on the sly to sip straight out of the bottle standing on a honey-colored wooden chest under a window which into this room, itself rather dark, admits a vision of green-striped golden hills under a pale blue sky; and in the storage building you enter from the village square, it's the odor, the chill and the enormous casks that a man could stand upright inside. In this chateau everybody lives from growing grapes and I learn about it little by little: the seed-beds and their seedlings which I am allowed to examine but not touch, the planting out, the sulphuring, the copper sulphate spraying. The vine-yards are different shades of green, depending upon the different sizes of the plants. And when the men are out dressing the vines we walk down the yellow dirt paths and bring them their lunch, a salad of white beans with garlic and sprinkled with parsley, the food in individual white crocks, a dish acting as protective lid for each and tied in place by means of a napkin, more white dishes, knives and forks and glasses in big white napkins and everything in baskets carried by us; and of course the harsh red wine that cannot be done without. And once you've brought their lunch to the men amidst the vines you stay to eat it with them, in the shade of trees surrounded by ochre hues, blue sky and golden light; then you bring back the baskets full of dirty dishes, empty crocks, used napkins. *You*, that is the women in the household, which includes me and, for a time, a companion of mine, a little dark-haired girl with eyes bluer than mine, who is hiding too but who still has her father and mother although they are not with us. I'd be very happy in this storybook castle if I knew where my mother was or at least if my aunt would stay with us for a little. But she brought me there and then went off right away, she is hiding somewhere else, in the home of a Protestant minister near Castres, she makes only brief appearances where we are and her going away leaves me in despair each time. One of these times I cry so hard and for so long that, throwing caution to the winds, she decides to stay one extra day. But something happens, a bridge is blown up, or some railroad tracks, and she is stranded with us for ten days or so. I am thrilled. I do not realize that it is dangerous, for her, for me, for the others. With my aunt there, part of my world has been restored to me; all is well.

Either then or at another time when she is staying with us a column of Germans shows up in the area. This time I am not frightened, I do not realize the danger, or else I have become fatalistic, or perhaps the worst I can conceive of, to lose my mother, has already come to pass. Our men head off into the vineyards. As for us, we shut the gates just beyond the drawbridge, and we wait behind our curtained windows. A car full of men in gray-green turns off the road and comes up the carriage-way towards the chateau, reaches the closed gates, pauses there for a moment, turns around, and drives off. Not until the end of the war am I to see any more Germans, and then it will be as prisoners, a line of blond men, stripped to the waist, sent to the Corrèze to work on the roads. However we have to wait until nightfall for the men who are protecting us to return from hiding.

In that chateau one day, just before the mid-day meal, I heard the Allied landing in Normandy announced over Radio London. That afternoon, bubbling over with joy, I danced and skipped along the pebbly road the whole way back from school. It was just under two months since my mother had been taken away and I almost think that it is to this news I owe the golden light which bathes all the memories I have of that end of spring, that beginning of summer, a moment for me at once fabulous and yet so very lonely. Fabulous, the chateau of porous gray stone against whose walls shrubberies rise and along whose exterior balconies run, connecting, at the height of the tree-tops, otherwise inaccessible chambers and nooks. To reach the toilets you follow one of those balconies and end up in a little room perched in the air above foliage and lodged in an angle; farther on the other balcony, of handsome wrought iron like this one, is considered unsafe and we children are not allowed to venture upon it. In this aerial outhouse, oh surprise! the pine seat has two holes, side by side, each provided with a lid you lift off before sitting down. When we both have to go, Elizabeth and I, we take our places next to each other and if it is night-time we peer at each other in the dark while waiting for nature to take its course. Apropos of two-holers I overhear some adult conversations centering upon the former bishops of Auch and Pope Joan. All this, of course, is definitely over my head. But that makes no difference: I take it all in, ask no questions, the words etching themselves in my memory.

And when I resift this whole period I am struck by the silence I maintained, I wonder at my capacity for asking no questions, at my ability to bounce from place to place and land intact in each, quickly picking up in one school where I left off in the last, receiving kindness first from these strangers and then from those, and at all times, just as on the first day when I listened to the clock tick above the white expanse of the big bed I had never been in before, dumbstruck, incapable of a word or a gesture, unable to let out a cry, unable to shed a tear in public, unable to talk about my mother and to ask grown ups whether they thought I would ever see her again. And what if my mother were to disappear forever the way my father had already done? Sometimes, without clearly formulating them to myself, I have moments of deep despondency that I do not disclose to others: at such times the only feeling left in me is of that loss, the so urgent need of my mother's lovingness that I cannot possibly have, and the painful feeling of the great lump in my throat, of the tears I am holding back. Among other such times I remember once standing by myself on the erstwhile drawbridge, gazing at the yellowish gravel on the ground and the brilliant pink flowers clinging to the gray stone buttresses, and I remember being submerged by woe, by my need to wrap myself up inside that blond and protecting tenderness, and clenching my fists from thinking about my mother and from controlling the awful lump in my throat. I would distill my unhappiness, my nostalgia to the point where I could not bear them any longer. The rest of the time I think about other things, I absorb myself in the beauty of what there is to see, in the light, in the smells. Sometimes too the memory of her steals up and takes me unawares. But never do I cry audibly, never do I ask questions about her future or mine. On that April morning, time, for me, came to an abrupt standstill, and since then I have huddled up and let myself be shuttled here and there, transplanted, reacclimated, passing without difficulty from one school to another and then to a third, without overmuch surprise or recalcitrance being introduced to other, contradictory ways of life fundamentally unlike mine, unlike ours–first of all, the gray, dismal miserliness of an old couple who hard up though they are do not hesitate to include me at their meager table, to install for me a third bed in the room where their grandchildren sleep, and from what little clothing those grandchildren possess to put together for me a wardrobe that in my opinion is plain and patched but which is interesting all the same, and very useful to me too and also covers the bareness of the shelf which together with the bed is, as of the first evening, designated as *my* part of the room we three share; and now, after those old people and their poverty, the opulence, the splendor that attach to ancient stone, to vineyards, to land, and

which add an unusual lustre to theaplate of spaghetti
and bean salad constituting our usual fare. There I
become acquainted with true luxury, finding it wonderful indeed but no more surprising than the shabbi-
ness in the gloomy, smoke-blackened quarters of the
watchman at the rear of the gray, walled-in courtyard.
While my sensitivity increases tenfold, nothing, on the
other hand, causes me surprise since that morning in
early April, the month I have my birthday in, when my
mother went away after promising she'd soon be back
to get me. But instead of coming back to where she had
left me she returned to our house to pick up some
forgotten piece of paper or to say something to the girl
who was acting as our maid, and I simply saw no more
of her–after having narrowly missed meeting her at
school (which accounted for the silence when I got
there) where in my classroom there were, in addition to
my usual classmates, all the girls from the classroom
across the hall; and their teacher had taken me by the
shoulders and turned me in the opposite direction
when the weight of that silence and of that wall of
staring eyes had brought my carefree progress to a
crashing halt: I had stood there for an unending instant,
stock still, attentive, contemplating the rectangular
patches of clear sky through the very high windows
below which were grouped all those incredulous gazes
fastened upon me. And then, as one might do to an
objcct, those hands turned me gently but firmly about
and started me moving in the opposite direction and I
quickly and obediently went that way, straight ahead,
without as yet grasping what had just happened to me

or understanding who was on the other side of the hallway, in Madame Nair's suddenly requisitioned classroom, at that moment denying my presence in an attempt to save my life. Had I, at that moment, realized she was there, so very near, I would probably have rushed toward her unthinkingly, as I used to do when vaccinations were administered in that same room. We would be marched two abreast across the hallway to be scarified and I would be bursting with pride to see my mother there, clad in a white coat and redolent of ether–a smile, a kiss won in the middle of the school-day afternoon, irruption into that well-ordered world of a bit of the unexpected, and how it would fill me with joy; the same as when sometimes, in the middle of the morning or the afternoon, the teacher would send me out to look at the big clock in the tower, thus enabling me to discover that the outside world went on existing even when I wasn't there and that on a week-day, while I was in school, outside the school people were walking across the broad village square, were shopping at the grocer's, coming and going at the adjoining barbershop, heading back toward the pharmacist's whose windows, between two translucent pear-shaped vessels, bore an inscription stating that he was a 1ST CLASS PHARMACIST, to my wondering eyes a formula both impressive and inscrutable. And over and above the delight of seeing what other people were up to when I was ordinarily somewhere else there was the pride of being the only one in my class who could tell time. Like the pride, when there were vaccinations, of being the only one whose mother came right into the school on official business during school hours, none of the three teachers having any children of her own. And now I also find myself–although I am not aware of it, and even were I aware of it I would not understand what it means–the only one here whose mother, at once Jewish and a member of the Resistance, is getting ready to experience the hell of the extermination camps.

Never during my life of hiding in what to me are foreign regions do my thoughts return to that morning, but sometimes I set myself to remembering my mother, or imagining her, to see how much I can bear of her fictive presence–which renders her real absence more unbearable still. Sometimes I evoke her boots, her shining black boots climbing up the narrow path from the garage behind our house, and also her doctor's satchel, the pebble-grained dull black leather satchel she is carrying. Sometimes I raise my eyes to include her coat, black also, a dull black, rough to the touch, standing out against the delicate green of the grass and against the bluer and darker green of the thuyas. Only rarely does my glance venture all the way up to her head, to her wavy blond hair, her pink cheeks, her smile, her dark brown eyes. Whenever I dare look that far up the lump forms in my throat, it scalds, it hurts. My eyes remain motionless and dry, I stiffen, I stand there; I am swept by a flood of grief, of nostalgia, but all that outpouring remains concealed, those tears of mine, that despair, a great inner burning, a great bitterness. The rest of the time, I play, I look at the world about me, I breathe it in, I am filled with wonder.

I'm sure that I also apply myself, for I go to school and I get good marks. But none of that has stuck in my memory, the one image I have being of the chickens pecking in the courtyard when I danced the whole way home the afternoon when, out of the blue, the radio reported Allied troops getting a foothold on our soil in Normandy.

On that day my doubts cease, hope returns, exuberance with it: the Allies have landed and I shall see my mother again. Perhaps that is how I manage to put up with her not being there, with the pain I feel, with my loneliness. It may be starting from that day I am able to let myself summon up before the eyes of my mind and of my heart the image of my perhaps not forever lost mother. Now and then, at moments when I feel very strong, I give measured expression to my sufferings. I never truly become very strong; but I learn to know that I am in pain, I learn to give measured release to the corrosive tears I have choked back. Fortunately for me, I do not know that for her the horror is only beginning; that this is the beginning for her of the humiliation, the hunger, the roll-calls standing unaided hour after hour outdoors, anyone unable to keep on his feet going straight to his death; hunger, dysentery, the body fading away, on certain days the windborne stink of burnt flesh settling over the camp and taking away the appetite of these famished women who have nothing to eat; the hunger, the thirst, the rain, the cold, the snow and no covering to wear during the roll-calls, standing there by the hour, weak from starvation, knees ready to buckle and the thought in your head that you've got to stay upright if you are ever going to come home; the hunger, the thirst, the cold, the sickness, the death all around you, staring you in the face, reeking in your nostrils, present everywhere as reality and as imminent danger, and the will to survive, to return, to help others do the same. And simultaneously the idea of her human dignity, affirmed with a force stronger than their systematic effort to dehumanize. Just as on the first day of her arrival at the camp she instinctively saw that it was better to walk than to avow her fatigue, and thereby saved her life, now she affirms, in the teeth of the exterminatory mechanism, that there are appearances to be maintained, that one must strive to keep clean or at least seem to be clean notwithstanding the lack of water and the absence of soap (and had they given her some bars of soap she could not have taken it upon herself to use them, made as they were from human fat extracted from human corpses), that one must tidy the lice-infested tufts of hair growing back on one's scalp, despite the lack of a brush or comb; and when in Canada (the term they use for the center where objects and clothing are sorted), when by way of thanks for a kindness rendered, a wound bandaged, some rest permitted upon a hospital bedstead, she is asked what she would like in return, as a gift, as a luxury, it is always a comb she requests and she has those half-dead women take turns using it, trying, with a view to escaping an impending selection, to have them reassume a human look. And when everything else has failed, when those entering the hospital too far outnumber those who are being discharged from it,

then it is to her force of persuasion she resorts in order
to get the dying onto their feet: *Up, you are going to get
up, you are going to arise and walk!* She does not save
them all; from time to time she saves one. But in order
to keep on struggling she refrains from thinking in
strictly numerical terms, and continues to wage the
same battle over and over again. Saves one; loses three;
saves another again. Thirty years later, by which time
I am older than she had been in those days and she has
long since stopped talking about her experience as a
deportee, a chance encounter brings up the memory of
something she had never mentioned hitherto. And she
tells of the death of a woman at Birkenau under
conditions so atrocious that the usual death from
starvation, from exposure, from exhaustion or else
from gassing or quicklime seems mild by comparison.
Thirty years have passed and today she weeps as she
tells the story of that mangled corpse, as if for her now
as once upon a time for me in my dream castle the day
I heard about the Allied landing, the ban against giving
way to emotion has at last been lifted; as if she too had
been inwardly paralyzed by the savagery of what was
done; as if in order to hold on she had had to forbid
herself all registering, all acknowledging of the horror,
the whole of her clenched through and through in that
life and death struggle, in her own behalf and in behalf
of others, a contracture, a knot which had persisted for
years and years in the stories told night after night in
her customary voice and without any perceptible feeling, as if horror were to be taken for granted (and that
is what I must have thought then) or as if (and it is

today, as I write, that I am elaborating this idea), as if the effort had been too great, her mobilization for survival too rigid, the anaesthetizing of her sensibility too entire, for her to be able–simply at will and simply because she had made her way back–to find in herself and transmit an emotion whose denial alone had enabled her to get back and to help some others get back alive.

As for me, one fine day before the so eagerly awaited period of grape-harvest, my aunt came to fetch me and after a stay of perhaps a month in Toulouse, where we learned of the death of her brother-in-law, shot by a firing squad outside the walls of the city, she took me back to my home in Corrèze, to my house of gray granite, to my garden, to my village, back to the green uplands of the Monédières, those meadows and chestnut groves where the ledge here and there breaks through the soil, that landscape without claim to grandeur or gloriousness but which is gentle and familiar and which up until now is the only one I can call mine. In my muddy village there once again is the road which brings you at last to the big central square where the school and the town hall are, there is the robust, square-built house again, its neat garden in front, its beaten earth courtyard in back and the kitchen-garden above; there is the path that comes up from the garage and upon it I sometimes visualize the black boots and the pebbly leather satchel until the hot lump in my throat gets near the point of bursting. There too is my grandmother, once again installed in her room looking out on the courtyard, looking out on the meadows, out there where the Upper Road starts, the Upper Road on which not so long ago they waited to no purpose in the clumps of trees just past the curve. There too is the presence of my aunt who sleeps in the big bed opposite mine. We came back to Chamberet a little after the opening of the school year and the first Thursday, chatting over the garden wall, I find out that all my friends have gone a grade ahead and are now in the upper classroom. As for me, I'm told I'm still with the middlers; my response to this news is an access of mute despair: in this awful business I have not only lost my mother but my friends as well, friends I was devoted to, friends I had vied with. The next day I too am promoted to the upper classroom: that's a lot better, the sun comes out again.

Among the uppers there is a stranger from a nearby village, a girl dressed all in black. Her blouse is black, so is her sweater, so are her shoes, she has dark hair, dark eyes; her face is broad and pale and altogether without expression. My friends take me to see her and we are formally introduced to each other. She does not say anything, she stares at me and her big brown eyes convey nothing. Later I learn that in the village where her home was the same Germans who arrested my mother several days later shot her father, and her mother, and a brother of hers, and a sister. It was done in front of her. She was underneath the bed, or else behind the door with a younger brother. Neither of them was hit. Now they live here, with an uncle and aunt who took them in. Both children have the same vacant gaze, the same colorless features, the same black clothing. She says little, she never smiles, she does her lessons with regularity, she walks without making any noise and moves down the aisle without touching the desks on either side. Her parents however weren't Jews or foreigners or in the Resistance: they were merely at home, their front door open, when the sowers of death rolled through. How had it happened? A question they failed to understand and did not reply to? A misinterpreted gesture? A weapon that goes off by itself in a hand tensed by the desire to kill? I am offered no explanation, if explanation my schoolmates have, who got their version of the story from their parents, who in turn got theirs from Yvette's uncle and aunt, who got theirs from the neighbors or from the child, stunned like the rest. But they were ordinary Correzians, without anything qualifying them as the targets of German vindictiveness. No explanation is forthcoming, and I do not ask for one. I accept the incomprehensible. I do not believe that I ponder things at the time and see how much worse this girl's fate is than mine. I do not become particularly attached to Yvette, who attaches herself to no one. Back again with my former classmates, warmth returns to me; we talk, we play, we try to outdo one another in school. Life becomes normal. I begin again to hope.

To negotiate also, and to interrogate signs. For hours on end I toy with the numbers I trace on paper. Certain numbers bring me hope, others cause me to cry, especially 2, which, drawn in a certain way, with a rather loosely rounded loop at the bottom, succeeds in reminding me of my mother, of her wavy blond hair, her tall, supple figure. I do not question that obscure connection; I accept it, turn it into a game, I keep my inward tears in check, bearing down on myself as hard and long as I possibly can. Often too I propose deals to the recently discovered Almighty who is perhaps hope but whose embodiment, for me, is the god the Catholics worship: *Make her come back even if she has to be a sourpuss and mean; I won't say anything if she's mean so long as she comes back; make her come back.* Behind this did there lie some adult conversation I could have overheard? In any case, it's all fantasy: the war is still not over, up until now nobody has seen a deportee return.

According to my recollection, that autumn, that winter were rainy beyond belief. I have no memory of lovely snowfalls, whereas, in the past, winter used to mean village and countryside underneath a deep blanket of dazzling crystalline whiteness through which, following the exact middle of the road, we would trample a path that to me at the time represented a colossal undertaking. Did the snow come up to my knees, or did I sink in to the height of an adult's knee? The path zigzagged down the center of the road, to left and right extended the pure white roadside, untouched; going to school became an adventure and coming home even more of an adventure. For as soon as the first flakes were on the ground the boys were waiting for us girls at the exit, to put snow down our necks and wash our faces with it. Whence our alarms, our secret consultings, our squeals, our thrills and delights. By and by the teachers react, from now on school ends for the girls five minutes before the boys are let out: and that puts a stop to those squeals, alarms and joys. But never mind, there will be others. And as those winters are severe, I have chilblains on my fingers and big toes. To take care of that my mother knits me some maroon-colored woollen wristlets that I wear all the time. The wool is a bit scratchy and they leave the ends of my fingers exposed; my fingers remain swollen but the skin cracks less. As for my toes, they go on swelling and itching, interminably. Upon my return to Chamberet I find the wristlets have vanished along with many other things, my pink tourmaline medallion and its gold chain, trinkets, objects. Little does it matter. They aren't my essential loss.

That winter I am often sick. The old doctor who comes from Treignac has a face covered with brown splotches. To examine me he lays a towel on my chest and then lays his face on top of it. Right in front of my eyes are the brown splotches, his wrinkled old skin, a grimy ear full of white hairs, and filling my nostrils is his rancid odor, a mixture of sweat and juice from the bottom of a pipe. I don't like him at all. I'd trade him for my mother any day. He prescribes cataplasms which effectively burn my back and enfold me in the pungent, clinging smell of mustard. I get better. I relapse. I'd take my mother any day; the treatment she used was never disagreeable. I don't like his flat finger-tips with his wrecked fingernails. I finally get well. Were it not that he usurped my mother's job I'd forgive him his aroma, his griminess: his eyes are calm and kindly, his touch is gentle, he ends up ridding me of my bronchitis. Where is my mother who was always neat and clean and good-smelling, who would get me well without having to bathe me in awful smells and burn the skin off my back?

The winter and then the spring came and went without leaving any particular impression upon me, whereas of the autumn that preceded them, the autumn of my return to Chamberet, I have memories of some wonderful things. As it turns out, they are in every case memories—and this is for me most significant although it had not occurred to me until this moment—, they are all memories of people coming from afar, as if these sudden arrivals, these unforeseen, sometimes humorous reappearances were but portents of the one great return which interested me. Thus there arrives a friend of my aunt, a Danish woman, horsey, wearing hobnailed boots and a khaki outfit, and as gifts she brings an enormous mushroom picked along the way and two huge yellow *pamplemousses*, whose name and taste I discover with delight. Never, in this land of the boletus and the chanterelle, have we seen a mushroom of such proportions; but since Jeanne proudly declares that it is edible we cook it and then, since I must eat promptly in order to get back to school, everyone sits down at table somewhat earlier than usual and we fall to, having decided that we all of us come through unscathed or else drop dead together. We do not drop dead. Jeanne was right, her big teeth gleam up there on the heights where her broad smile and friendly eyes preside. She spends the evening bathing her feet, for she walked to get here, twenty,

twenty-five kilometers, why, she had a great time of it the whole way, it's terrific to be back together again, now that the war's over in our part of Europe. Then, after two or three days, she's off again, scarf wound round her neck, cap over one ear. The next to arrive is my aunt, after bicycling from Treignac, having got there I've no idea how for she had come from Paris. The last time I had seen her was in Toulouse, she had laughed and cried both at once, had told about her forced residence in the Vaucluse and the bus ride up to Paris under German escort. She had brought me, wonder of wonders! a bracelet chain made of the Allies' different flags connected by gold links. This time, true fairy godmother that she is, she takes from her bag three persimmons which I gobble up before she has a chance to tell me that they aren't ripe and that I must wait. No waiting for me! I can't resist green fruit and in the days of my mother and father I would make thorough raids upon the still unripe currants and gooseberries, causing my perplexed mother to wonder why those bushes produced so little. And then the day of my horrified encounter with that thing wound once, twice, three times, four times around the slender stalks, that interminable pearl-gray gartersnake, its round head thrust toward me. Instantaneous right about face on my part, shrieks that roused the entire household; and therewith ceased the infertility of those fruit bushes. That, all that was before.

Another time, we return home from an afternoon walk: the neighbors inform us that while we were gone two young women drove up in a military truck and wanted to speak to my grandmother. We wait a little and back they come, fair-haired, pink-faced, well-fed, in uniform. I have a confused memory of a procession of military vehicles. But that may only be an extension of the procession of packages they produce from within that canvas-covered truck, thirty-seven at least and maybe forty-eight cardboard boxes filled with foreign victuals which the British Red Cross, concerned for the welfare of His Majesty's subjects, is having delivered to my grandmother now that she can be reached; the whole representing the exact total of packages that ought normally to have kept her from perishing of hunger during the war. That is when, surprised and indignant, I discover the mixture of pork and pineapple in cans from Australia; and, a little after, contrive to chew, without being able to get the better of, a thin strip of rubbery stuff, initially sweet but soon tasteless— and, not knowing what else can be done with it, swallow it, I being a properly brought up little girl who does not spit out something she has had in her mouth. Vociferous adults nearby endeavor to explain to me that chewing gum is to be chewed and not swallowed.

On the whole those days are not sad, they are just dull. I have my grandmother and my aunt back again, I have my house again, where the only thing missing is the center of my life; I have my school again, my school-friends. I do my schoolwork, do it pretty well, with elaborate systems for copying, my book open upon my knees, when we do the maps of the colonies. I am now one of the uppers, in the room all the way to the right when you look at the school from the outside.

Like the other two classrooms it has three tall windows on either side, and for heating in the winter, a big cast-iron stove with a pipe that meanders this way and that. As in the past, when we arrive we take off our wooden sabots and remain in the socks we wear inside those sabots. Also as in the past, in winter, we bring to school little bags of boiled chestnuts in whose shell we poke a little hole and suck out the soft and sweet inside during recreation. As in the past we play tag and hopscotch and we make up rounds and sing them. We also do a great deal of talking and we conduct disputes from opposite ends of the courtyard through the intermediary of messengers who assist first the one side and then the other in finding potent insults when the aggrieved parties' imaginations give out. But though similar in every point to what it had been before, this life nevertheless lacks the magic of new discoveries: the first wild games of tag on the concrete ledge topped by wire fence which separates the courtyard where we play from the garden reserved for the teachers; the little chrysanthemums poking through the fence, the dark, prettily shaped chrysanthemum leaves that I crush between my fingers for the sake of the strong odor; during the first game of tag, those earliest breakneck dashes across the courtyard to the safety, on the farther side, of a broad, gradual stairway leading nowhere; the first attentions of those girls who from strangers are due to turn into my closest friends (*She doesn't know the game yet, let's give her another chance . . .*). Lacking above all else is my mother, at noontime, at four o'clock when I go home, and in the morning when I get up.

In my class, in the upper grade, there is another girl who is always dressed in black. Her name is Georgette and I know her well. I knew her father and mother well too, when they used to run the big grocery store on the other side of the square. Her father, with retreating curly black hair and always wearing a gray smock, used to talk to my mother at great length. Our families didn't visit on Sundays but there was a kind of friend-ship or fraternal spirit between her father, a Socialist mayor before the war, and my mother and Georgette's mother, a slow-moving, somewhat heavy woman who wore her dark hair looped up loosely on either side of her lovely serene face. Now Georgette is left, along with her mother, still slow-moving and somewhat heavy and these days dressed all in black, and a little boy, a younger child. To help with the store there is also a tiny grandmother, the mother of Georgette's father. As for him, he disappeared together with one of the schoolteachers in the settling of scores that took place in the village right after the Liberation. They went off in a delivery van one late afternoon upon the summons of a fellow belonging to a different under-ground faction from theirs: *So-and-so wants to have a word with you.* The message was addressed to Mous-son, the grocer. The teacher read it and thought it looked fishy: *Just a second, I'm coming with you,* and he got into the van without even crossing the square to tell his wife he was going. They did not return that evening, they did not return the next day, nor the day

after that. A search was made in the surrounding hills
and their bodies were found a few days later in a ditch,
lying side by side, together in death as they had been as
partisans fighting to free their country. And now Madame Nair, my teacher of the previous year, she who
took hold of my shoulders amidst the silence and
without a word turned me around and despatched me
from that danger-fraught classroom, she who the previous year, before all these events, had had such fun
training us to distinguish between the *é* of the past
tense and the *è*-sound of the imperfect in order that we
avoid errors in dictation, now Madame Nair is also all
in black. She doesn't smile anymore, her wide mouth
sags at the corners. I'm glad I'm in another class, I'm
glad I've got a different teacher: I prefer Mademoiselle
Laivost in spite of the stoop in her shoulders. During
that winter, during that spring, I wait. . . Time takes
forever to pass.

5

My father.

One day, a day no different from any other day, he set off as he set off every day; but on that day he didn't come back.

My father. He had taught me how to tell time, by means of a sheet of cardboard where in blue ink he had printed the twelve numerals and with a bent pin affixed two moveable hands likewise of cardboard and each ending in an arrowhead, the longer of the two hands all but covering up the numbers it was supposed to point to. It is to this knowledge I got from him that when school resumed in the autumn following his death and I was placed right away in the advanced group of the lowers because I already knew how to read and write well enough not to have to start with beginners; it is to this knowledge that I owed the privilege, during that last of the peaceful years, being

the only one who could tell time in that class of little
girls where the oldest was perhaps seven; the privilege
of being allowed to leave the big classroom with the
twin sets of tall windows full of luminous panes
through which great spaces of sky appeared on the wall
to the right and on the wall to the left; of being allowed
upon occasion to leave that classroom in the middle of
the afternoon to find out what time it was by the clock
on the wall outside. A privilege it assuredly was, and I
was exceedingly proud of it; but in addition to that and
more important still it was the look I got at the rest of
the world at an hour and upon days when I never saw
it: mid-afternoon in the middle of the week.

At ten past three of a Tuesday or a Wednesday
(children's day off used then to be Thursday) the square
lay beyond the reach of my inquiring and supervisory
gaze, and it is a surprise to discover it flat and vacant
and immense, bordered by the usual shops, the grocery
with the timbered facade standing at the top of three or
four steps running the length of the storefront and
compensating the slope of the ground; the hairdresser
where my mother sometimes goes to have a wave put
in her hair or to have its blondness touched up at the
roots, for actually its real color is light brown; farther
on, beyond the street leading to the church, there
where my grandmother will soon be spending several
months, invisible and mute, hidden in the attic, farther
on is the pharmacist, former graduate of some provin-
cial school of pharmaceutical studies or other, whose
incomprehensible and therefore fascinating sign, hand-
lettered, flourishes between two mighty pieces of glass-

ware, pear-shaped bottles taller than I by far, one of them green, the other a purplish mauve, huge translucent candies or gems I'd like to be able to taste or bite into, and behind them a mysterious dispensary in whose depths strange things are floating in jars filled with greenish or yellowish fluids: here a foetus of uncertain form, there a serpent with black-and-gold scales, objects I avert my eyes from each time, although not before verifying that they are still there; still farther on, on the opposite side of the street leading to the fairgrounds, the hotel, an elongated building; then the shoemaker whose daughter with the two yellow braids is right now turning into my best friend. . . But at this point in my wondering investigation–the world exists independently of the gaze I bend upon it, and people go to the grocer's while I am at school and unable to see them–, an investigation that is certainly over with in less than the time I have taken to describe it now, I remember my errand, glance up, and hasten proudly back to advise the teacher that it is ten past three outside and that her wristwatch is therefore working correctly. A blessed year, my first year of school, a year I am sure I overrate, but which did bring me so many new experiences: new tastes, sights, odors. That big room with the tall windows letting in bright sky where, when I have finished my lesson, I look about and listen to the little ones learning to read letters and syllables displayed upon pages of stiff paper bound at the top like a pad of note-paper but cut vertically into three panels which can be lifted or lowered separately so that the letters on them can be combined into any number of syllables–*C A T* becomes *C A R* or *F A R* or *F A N*–; while on another pad syllables are combined into words. With the tip of a special rod the teacher flips up this or that panel in order to obtain, first in large bold letters, then in smaller, more slender ones, all sorts of combinations which with the gradual development of the pupil's perception and the increasing demands of the teacher or the more advanced pupil replacing her, finally form words full of meaning.

I know how to read and write. And though my still unsure hand produces inelegantly shaped letters I am deemed good enough to go straight into the advanced group, and there begins my wonderstruck initiation into the magical world, the world unto itself of school-book literature: *the sun-kissed grape, the bronzing leaves of autumntide, old garden walls 'rayed in the vine's new growth; the stolid oxen, patient and mild; the majestic progress of the sower advancing over the freshly turned field; the hoofs of the goat shining in the golden gorse; the windmill's sails in the gloaming; the belling of the stag, the howling of the wind,* and *the cosy hearth, warm and snug*–here fanciful and reality compose a blend that fuels the imagination and which is in near enough relation to the everyday country life I have recently discovered for my wonderment to be able to take root and include the plump new words that ring in my ear and suggest pictures to my mind; the reign of harmony, calm and justice to match the one that at home they hold up to me as the normal order of the world.

Sometimes we go on walks to collect chestnuts: we fill burlap sacks to the brim with them, they will be shipped to cities or to the armed forces, we aren't sure just which, but it is in connection with the war that we haven't yet experienced first-hand. And once we spend the morning bringing in the teachers' winter firewood supply: instead of going to class we file up the narrow stairway, a chunk of wood in either hand, while another file comes down, the panting, puffing, rollicking chain proceeding from courtyard to loft and on back to courtyard, each young human element imbued with the importance of the task and enormously enjoying–at least in my case–the extraordinary character of this school-day morning during which one can see what's going on outside all the while being inside.

But this period also has its hours of ignominy or of injustice. There is the day the first geography map comes, the day for reproducing the map of France. I, a cerebral youngster, hesitant of hand, sit helpless before the task until my mother shows me how to divide the country up into like-sized squares and to reproduce its outline, square after square, on a quadrille-ruled page of my school notebook. Which in no time results in an impeccable France and, the next day, when with justifiable pride I arrive at school, in the monstrous accusation of having traced my map, a serious offense in this establishment offering an at once manual, intellectual and moral apprenticeship. But we are still living in times when the righteous must prevail and when the morality I find in books and which my mother paints for me in glowing colors enables one to sift the good from the bad and vindicate the innocent. Right being on my side, I refer to my mother and to her scientific method of cartographic reproduction and with the teacher looking on, dumbfounded but willing to own her mistake, upon the blackboard which for the occasion I first rule off into regular squares, I reproduce the departments of Pas-de-Calais and then of the Manche. There I halt my demonstration. I emerge from the incident covered with glory and more than ever convinced that good faith and honesty can only win out.

Times bygone, passed very far away, simple wonders of the everyday, unrecapturable because that world exists no longer save inside me, where sometimes I try to bring it back to life. Very bygone times of wonderful childhood that I probably further embellish to offset or to deny the absence of him most passed away and gone of all, my father.

My father. Writing this text, my memory of him eludes me the way, I imagine, his presence, long ago, suddenly turned into absence. He must have left one ordinary morning as he did every day since his return from the *drôle de guerre*–sometimes patients to see in his office on the ground floor of our house, sometimes calls within a radius of several kilometers around Chamberet, having been obliged early on to give up the hard and fast schedule (consultations from 9:30 to 11:30, from 1:30 to 3:30, and by appointment) that the sign still spelled out in yellow letters against a black background on our front door when it was my mother who left, she herself having had no inkling of the chaos, the emergencies, the time spent on the road that a rural practice implies or implied then. Except, that day, he didn't come back. I don't even know whether we said goodbye that morning, whether we were cross with each other, whether I'd misbehaved, whether I'd been too busy playing, or whether on that particular day it just so happened that he was behind time or else called out on an emergency when he hadn't been expecting to have to leave. . . A little later I was in the kitchen, at table, having been put there and the door having been shut. I was chewing endlessly on a piece of what I had been told was eel. I can see myself sitting at the big round table with its oil-cloth cover, I see myself chewing and rechewing that tough, dry, bony morsel that wouldn't go down. Ordinarily I did not have my lunch in the kitchen but in the dining room together with my mother and grandmother, my father's mother. As for him, he would eat whenever he got back, at whatever hour it might be. Of that day, as for that matter of those preceding it, I have no remembrance, only the thought of that meal, of that eel which must have been holiday fare for eel was not a common item on our menu in that highland region, in that time of war. Between a morning departure I am reconstructing and that unswallowable mouthful of springy flesh crammed with little bones, I encloseted in the warm kitchen with our old servant, there is nothing, not a trace of a memory. I can only imagine his departure as having been perfectly everyday, perhaps without his saying goodbye to me, perhaps after a scolding or an unresolved quarrel, and then someone came to notify my mother that his car lay overturned in a pond.

In the town of Portes-en-Ré one night thirty years later I had just fallen asleep when I was awakened by the sounds of running feet in the darkness, a rapping at our door and a voice saying that a lady had to be told that her little girl had tumbled from a window. Once I'd realized it was the woman next door and not I, after having got up all the same, my heart racing, to make certain that my own daughter was quietly asleep in her bed where she was supposed to be, once reassured that they had the situation in hand, that the doctor was there, the rescue squad coming to take the child (quite unhurt, moreover) to the hospital, and sitting at my window contemplating the faintly lighted street where there were shapes stirring soundlessly, figures retreating, I told myself *I've been through this before,* but beyond a recognizable emotion and the tumult in my breast, I was unable to recapture the place, the time, the circumstances. It was long after the night in Portes that I thought of that first morning when somebody must have come to our door to tell my mother about my father's car lying overturned in a pond.

My father drove fast, a bit too fast I heard my mother say afterward. Apart from that, in this peaceful, undistinguished village of ours there was a man who, it would seem, did not hesitate to use his automobile to try to put his competitors or political rivals out of the way when he encountered them on the narrow and little traveled roads of this end of the plateau. Affidavits exist, and I have seen them, that tell of his car's unexplained swerves in the direction of certain pedestrians, always walking alone, always persons of another persuasion than his. Forcing his luck, did this man wait in his car beside a sharp bend in the road, then charge out at the oncoming vehicle, counting on the reflex of its driver who in an effort to avoid him would end up in the pond? I don't know and so I cannot say. But I do know that after the car had been pulled out of the pond–where it had lain upside down under the water, with, floating inside it, the lifeless body of my father who must have struck his head also–, I do know that it was he, that man, who was sent for, he, the same, who did not hesitate two and a half years later, when the opportunity arose, to give my mother away to the *Das Reich* officers, nor, my mother having been taken care of and the German defeat now a foregone conclusion, to switch sides, making some new friends in certain underground groups and using them at the Liberation for the assassination of his old political rival, Mousson, the grocer in the gray smock, socialist mayor during the Front Populaire, Resistance companion to my mother and to certain others.

After that morning, after that mid-day meal behind closed doors in the kitchen, I saw no more of my father until he was dead and I was carried into his room with my eyes closed; and when I was at last allowed to open them, there, in that dark room, illuminated by a single candle reflecting in a mirror, there was his wan profile above a colorless sheet.

6

One day, one fine day, she returned. That occurred, fittingly, in springtime, a little over a year after her arrest. First, I believe, came the armistice. Or the first deportees may have arrived a few days before that. I am hazy about the order of events then. But I clearly recall that as soon as the first of them began to arrive, as soon as lists were posted of the first survivors to get back, my aunt went up to Paris, to look and to wait. Or else we first had word that someone back from there had at some moment or other very definitely known her, alive, in an extermination camp. Maybe it was only then that my aunt went up to Paris. Or maybe she made two trips, maybe she went and then came back to tell us, my grandmother and me, that at a given point, as abstract as one of the givens in arithmetic problems in school, she had been seen alive, had been spoken to. Then went back to try to get news, as train after train came in looking for her husband's name and for her sister's, and then came back to Chamberet to tell me, this time, that she had turned up, was alive, mere skin and bones but alive, her eyes the same, her smile the same as ever.

Or at least they appeared unchanged to me, her eyes, her smile, owing to which I did not notice her fearful thinness, the absence of her long blond hair, ill replaced by short unkempt tufts full of large whitish nits. But little did it matter. She was back; and I had made so many bargains with the Catholic God, waiving her smile and her good mood ahead of time provided she return, be it in a bad temper and unkind. She was back, my heart's desire, my safety's guarantee, smiling and draped in a high-necked white nightgown, lying in a bed where she was to remain for the fourth part of a year, only to exchange that bed for another. But little did that matter either. She was back, just in time for her birthday and it was I who received a gift, *The Little Prince,* that I didn't like at the time, having understood neither the book's contents nor what she wrote in inscribing it to me–*After her miraculous escape from prison*–, not yet having begun to listen, night after night, year after year, to those obsessional stories of daily life in a German death-camp.

My present to her was a live duck which thrust its head out of the wicker basket and complained loudly the whole way up to Paris on the train, every clack of whose wheels underscored the one thought in my head: *I'm going to see Maman again, to see Maman again.* Back from twelve or thirteen months of fasting, she had expressed a wish for roast duck, and we had scouted out one for her and carried it with us on the bus, then on the train. And then put it for a swim in the bathtub in the Paris apartment where a friend of hers offered her a bed and in addition all of a true sister's affection. Until such time as she was up and about again. And as regards the duck, until such time someone appeared who could cut its throat and finally turn it into something edible. And when at last a slice of it was served to her she was unable to touch it, being too sick to take solid food, having lost a third of her former weight, her heart having enlarged by a half, and the rest of her organs being totally out of tune. And then they hospitalized her in an effort to save her, reduced as she was by twelve or thirteen months of deportation that had been succeeded by twelve or thirteen days of liberation when, once over their tremendous joy at being free again, and alive, and triumphant, those women discovered that nothing had been set up for the purpose of getting them home and they realized that if they wanted to return to their country they would have to do it on foot. On foot and by road, the way they had reached the camp, on foot and by road, as it had been during the withdrawal from Auschwitz, minus the snow.

In the final days of the war, in that quiet little everyday sort of camp in northernmost Germany where they had wound up after having been evicted from the overpopulated Ravensbruck where they had been permitted to stay for only a night or two, in this quiet little run-of-the-mill camp where they weren't undertaking to exterminate them systematically, where their captors were merely letting them starve to death, with the detachment and lassitude of an army due shortly to go down in defeat and conscious of it, they were liberated by Red Army elements totally unimpressed by their plight after all they had undergone themselves. And so there they were, free, on the side of the victors, still alive, but for want of food as famished as before. A day went by, then another. Then my mother, who spoke some Russian, betook herself to the commandant of the camp or rather of the armed forces that had charge of them now, and explained to him, in what she knew of his language, that they were perishing of hunger. Oh, but that wouldn't do. Everything would be taken care of. Altogether without ill-will but utterly devoid of imagination, the commandant dispatches two enlisted men who deliver an entire steer to them a few hours later. A dead steer, true enough, and skinned, but raw, intact, not cut up. And in that situation, the thought arose in my mother's mind automatically: how to keep them from giving way to their appetite as formerly she had had to keep them from yielding to their exhaustion. For these half-dead women what was needed was a cup of clear broth, a biscuit. I visualize my mother struggling to prevent her companions from hurling themselves on that food, talking to them about the end of their wanderings and their hardships and about their return home, within sight at last, in order that they not die there, die now, stupidly, from indigestion.

After that, calm. The war is over. But nothing happens. The Russians harbor no grievance against these women, but no place has been assigned to them within the overall scheme. Frenchwomen, oh yes. Dying, yes. Having, in their own way, won the war. But no plans exist for getting them home. Besides, they themselves, humble parts of a victorious Red Army, have paid a more than ordinary price to win this war. They have known the ravages of hunger, the cold that kills, battles. To these terribly beset women, their little French sisters in the struggle and in the victory, they offer the same indifference they maintain towards their own sufferings, their own dead–the same indifference that enabled them to keep going and to win.

A day passes, then another. If something is not done for these women they are going to die, these women who have come through, who are free, but so profoundly malnutritioned, devastated. Once again, in her sketchy Russian, which probably earns the man's respect, my mother addresses the commandant.

But you are quite free to go, he declares. *We aren't keeping you here.* He gestures toward the west, waves a hand in the direction of their homeland and above all in that of the American troops who, a few kilometers away, on the other side of the intermediary zone, have established an emergency air-lift to France. Free to go, indeed. But how? Not a word about a truck, a jeep. It is probably out of the question that the least thing be done that might be construed as having an official character. In the end they get hold of an ox-drawn cart and in it the weakest, the sickest are deposited. The others follow on foot, my mother in their midst, on foot as she was when she entered Birkenau, as she was when she made the interminable trek across a Germany soon to collapse but as yet holding together under its carapace of snow.

I know not what it required in time and courage for those exhausted women, convinced they could not take another step, nonetheless to traverse, unaided, on foot, in the war-shattered Germany of that spring, the not very many kilometers separating them from deliverance.

After that it was the return, the warm hospitality of a friend, our finding each other again. We are each all right, although in her case it may not be for long; but of this I am not aware. She is there, she is safe, and with nothing to worry about I can acquaint myself with this Paris where I was born but which is a foreign city to me and which during that torrid summer I discover by way of its scents and sounds: mingled odors of cooking and of floor-wax on the stairs of the Ninth Arrondissement apartment buildings, the less civilized effluvia surrounding an occasional G.I. sleeping it off in a doorway after a binge; the sound hitherto unknown to me of the morning garbage cans rattling in the courtyard, prelude to a rich and exciting daily hubbub. There were also the scraps with a band of boys a little older than I, punches received, tufts of hair pulled out; and the breathless dodging in and amongst the neatly trimmed shrubbery in the square to get a glimpse of the lovers who might be kissing there. And one day, crossing the rue de

Chateaudun, I nearly got myself run over. That indeed would have been a stupid thing to have happen.

For in the meantime on the bed in the hospital where she had been taken, she was fighting to recover. They had put her in the hospital to try to bring her heart back to normal proportions, to moderate its beat, to restore the internal equilibrium, the organization which provides for the correct functioning of the body. She was fighting for those things; fighting to extract nourishment from food, to end that intestinal debacle which was draining away her vital fluids; to set her system back on its tracks, to check infection. And to ensure that that perseverance, that struggle, this return had not been for nothing. And fighting alongside her was the doctor, a friend, who had made himself responsible for her life and who, unable to know what was going to happen—for they had not yet indexed these disorders caused by excesses of suffering along with subjection to cold, to famine, to that program of total dehumanization—, felt his way ahead, deliberated, shifted his approach, at last declared her out of danger. And also fighting at her side were her relatives, her friends who at a time of general shortage got hold of the antibiotic shots, those millions of units of the penicillin that was nowhere to be found and which they begged, borrowed and stole, and which saved her.

At last, in the fall, with school about to start, she was up again and able to leave for a rest in the country, in a convalescent home. For my part, I went back to my elementary school studies in Chamberet on my plateau in the Monédières.

When several months later we were brought back together again I found my mother anew and, at the same time, lost her. By then she was truly out of danger, but the effects of edema had more surely destroyed the harmony of her features than had the dreadful thinness which had reduced her to a pair of eyes and a smile. Seeing her again, it took me a few seconds to recognize my mother in this lady who made happy gestures and laughed while she gazed at me. Furthermore, she was accompanied by a man I wasn't much bothered about at first but whom I later on began to hate passionately once I understood that he was going to encumber our lives forever.

The war was over. Neither of us was dead. We were living together in the same house, we loved each other. But over the course of those months I had somehow turned irrevocably into an adult. From then on it was incumbent upon me to protect my mother who had come close to dying and who would remain fragile for a long time, at least so we anticipated. Henceforth it would be mine to become the monument that endures and that for the span of a human lifetime maintains the memory of him who was my father, whom she had–I then believed–forgotten or betrayed. Henceforth it would be mine to listen in order to become imbued with her stories, without yet knowing that this inges-tion preluded another task: that of speaking, for her and in her name, about the unspeakable that she had had the strength both to live through and to vanquish but which she would not be able to bring herself to consign to words intended to remain, relying instead upon oral tradition and for its preservation upon this link to the future sprung from her, who has now assumed her mission.